THE GRE___ ___OK ___

Pears

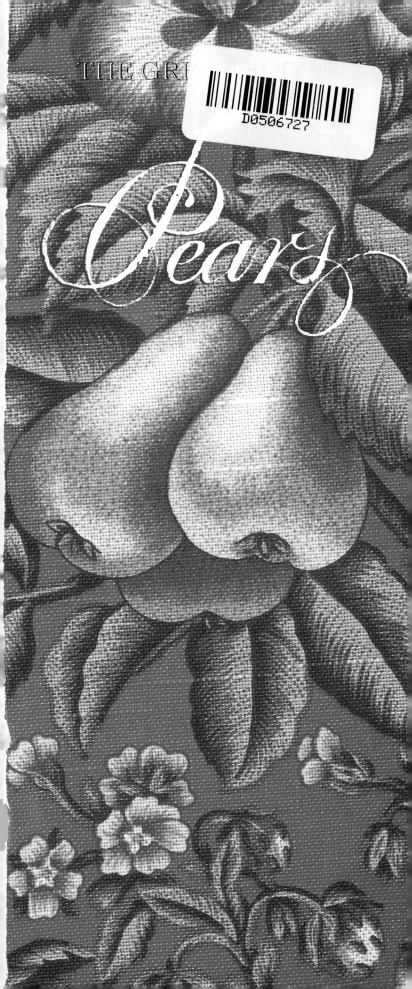

THE GREAT BOOK OF

Pears

BARBARA JEANNE FLORES

PRINCIPAL PHOTOGRAPHY BY SUSANNE KASPAR

Ten Speed Press

Berkeley Toronto

1⊜

Ten Speed Press
P.O. Box 7123
Berkeley, California 94707
www.tenspeed.com

Distributed in Australia by Simon and Schuster Australia, in Canada by Ten Speed Press Canada, in New Zealand by Southern Publishers Group, in South Africa by Real Books, in Southeast Asia by Berkeley Books, and in the United Kingdom and Europe by Airlift Books.

Design by Barbara Flores
Production by Lisa Patrizio and Stephanie Fitz Ariel

Background Art on cover is *Villa Cicogna, Bisuschio,* by Maxfield Parrish, from the 1904 edition of *Italian Villas and their Gardens* by Edith Wharton.

Library of Congress Cataloging-in-Publication data
Flores, Barbara, 1948–
      The great book of pears / Barbara Jeanne
      Flores ; photography by Suzanne Kaspar.
        p.   cm.
      ISBN 1-58008-036-7 (paper)
      1. Pear. 2. Pear—Varieties. 3. Cookery (Pears) I. Title.
SB373. F59   1999   99-32089
634'.13--dc 21   CIP

First printing, 2000
Printed in (Hong Kong)

1 2 3 4 5 6 7 8 9 10 — 04 03 02 01 00

To Jaime,
a fruit grower and a gentleman,
and my husband of twenty-five years.

And to the Filoli Estate,
for preserving their heritage pear collection
for future generations.

CONTENTS

BY
LINDSEY REMOLIF SHERE

When I was twelve, my parents moved from Chicago to a ranch in California's Sonoma County, where fresh fruit was plentiful and Bartlett pears grew among peaches, nectarines, plums, and cherries in the family orchard. Since I was the oldest of five girls and did not like working in the dairy, helping to cook for the family fell on my shoulders. I baked constantly—cakes and pies and cookies. I don't even remember what all, but my sister tells me she was tired of having to eat all those cakes.

When Chez Panisse opened almost thirty years ago, I knew that supermarket fruit was only a caricature of the fruit I had grown up with. Once you have tasted a pear picked from the tree and properly ripened, a pear that doesn't have to be shipped anywhere, you will know there is no comparison. The White Doyenné, for example, is delicious, rich, winelike, and melting, but it can't be found at a supermarket because it doesn't ship from California to New York. Even at Chez Panisse, we haven't had the luxury of using heirloom variety pears like the Doyenné, because they aren't available to us.

To find good pears, go to local farmers' markets and ask to taste. There are many different pears, with a wide variety of flavors, outside of the supermarket. A really good pear reminds me of wine: complex, sensuous, and strongly perfumed.

Once ripe, pears are a fragile fruit. Either we buy perfectly ripe pears for the restaurant to use that day, or we buy them and ripen them ourselves for later use. We use Comice a lot. A properly ripened Comice is the most delicious pear, with a sweet, juicy, complex flavor. The most wonderful caramel pears you can imagine are made by combining Comice juices with the melted sugar; it's beyond the sum of its parts. Comice bake well and make wonderful sherbets, but we don't poach them because they are so fragile. Boscs, however, with their beautiful elongated necks, are excellent poached whole in red or white wine or muscat grape juice. Pretty little Seckels we poach with their colorful skins on. We also use Winter Nélis quite often for baking and sherbets, but we never get a big supply. French Butter pears and summer Bartletts are also favorites. D'Anjou? I had one delicious d'Anjou once, and it was an organic one. So I know they can be good.

I hope tasting a really delicious pear may inspire people to plant their own tree. It's worth the five- to six-year wait (see page 155 for mail-order suppliers). Even in a small yard you can grow several different varieties, especially if you espalier trees along a fence or walkway in the classic European tradition. We had a dwarf Comice in our small Berkeley backyard that gave us three full boxes of delicious pears year after year.

When we started Chez Panisse, we went to local growers looking for foods that tasted good to us, that had a quality we couldn't get at the supermarket. At first, people thought we were just interested in baby greens, but it is so much more than that. It's about finding locally grown foods, tasting what we find and living and eating sustainably. Alice [Waters] is an incredibly gifted spokeswoman for these ideals. People think organic food is too costly and that cooking takes too much time. But if you taste, really taste, and think, everything will have its proper balance. When people taste the difference they will want the superior quality of fruit that organic farming can produce.

Lindsey Remolif Shere is one of the owners of Chez Panisse in Berkeley, California, and was its pastry chef for twenty-six years.

White Doyenné

IN SEARCH OF THE
WHITE DOYENNÉ

s one supermarket shopper put it, "There are pears that taste like shampoo, and there are those that don't." So what's so great about pears?

My interest in pears started because they were beautiful. As a graphic designer, I was attracted to their sensuous feminine shapes and rich Renaissance colors. Lined up at the camera's-eye level, pears look like interesting strangers sitting at a bus stop, more revealing than the standard looking-down-at-a-plate shot. So photographer and dear friend Susanne Kaspar and I hunted up unusual varieties, primarily looking for pears with leaves still on the stem.

Following a lead on heirloom pears, I drove to Filoli, a historic estate south of San Francisco. On arriving, I was directed to the back room of the visitor's center, where nearly a hundred boxes of carefully arranged pears were sitting up awaiting the next day's public pear-tasting event (that pear tasting was an event seemed a novel idea). The boxes were labeled Louise Bonne d'Avranches and Duchesse d'Angoulême, names not likely to be found at a supermarket or a bus stop.

An overwhelming perfume filled the room—luscious, provocative, reminiscent of a musky wine cellar, yet lighter and sweeter. I observed that Filoli's horticulture director, Lucy Tolmach, was very protective of her fruit. "Be careful. These Louise Bonnes are delicate. They bruise easily," she said. "We can only spare one or two."

According to Filoli instructions, I wrapped my samples in a paper bag and labeled it. Having loaded my precious cargo of twenty or so pears for the shoot, I realized how hungry I was. The aroma from the back seat filled the car. "Maybe we wouldn't miss just one."

I picked up a small yellow pear shaped like a little turban that yielded slightly to my touch. The bag read White Doyenné. I bit into it. It melted in my mouth. The taste was more like a fine, rich, buttery chardonnay than any pear I had tasted. Like wine, it was sweet yet tart, with musky undertones and a strong perfume. Never in my life had I tasted fruit like that! I had eaten good, juicy peaches from a Georgia fruit stand and wonderful mangoes on a stick in Mexico, but nothing like this. "This is like a fine chardonnay," I thought, with juice dribbling down my chin.

After the shoot, when the last treasured pears had been devoured within feet of the camera and the feast was over, we eagerly asked Lucy, "Where can we buy these?" The disappointing answer was that we had to wait until next year's tasting at Filoli. Being used to getting fruit year-round at the supermarket, it was an odd yet enticing feeling knowing that I'd have to wait another whole year until October to taste the juices of a White Doyenné. I was beginning to understand what all the hoopla was about.

Author Barbara Flores and a Filoli volunteer taste heirloom pear varieties at Filoli Fall Festival.

History

Monticello (Thomas Jefferson's
Virginia Estate and fruit
orchard)

THE FRUIT OF THE GODS

Native to temperate Europe and Western Asia, pears (*Pyrus communis*) are one of the two dozen plants known to have been cultivated for over 4,000 years. According to historians, the fruit is likely to have originated in the South Caucasus, North Persia, or the Middle East and found its way into Egypt and Europe. Dried "cultivated" slices were discovered in the cave dwellings of the Ice Age in Switzerland. In the fourth century B.C., ancient Greek authors had detailed information about the propagation of pears, which Homer called "the fruit of the gods." During the years when Socrates wandered the streets of Athens, and Euripides, Sophocles, and Aeschylus wrote the classic Greek plays, wealthy Greeks dined on delicious cultivated pears like the ancient Jargonelle. The Athenian peasant, however, living in the countryside, subsisted on roots, nuts, an occasional grasshopper, figs, and wild, rocklike pears.

The Romans, with their passion for the exotic, brought back from Greece not only art and architecture, but also delicious fruits. They ended lavish meals with bowls of grapes, apples, and pears. Many of the best Roman pear varieties survived for a thousand years in Italy, until the Renaissance, when even better varieties were developed. Six varieties of pear are recorded

THE PARTRIDGE IN THE PEAR TREE

The traditional Christmas carol, "The Twelve Days of Christmas," which mentions a gift of a partridge roosting in a pear tree, is said to be of French origin. In the Middle Ages, the pear was a phallic symbol, and the partridge a notorious emblem of lust. To give a partridge in a pear tree to one's beloved suggests intentions beyond garden decor. Also, an old yuletide custom of walking around a pear tree three times was said to bring a vision of one's beloved.

as being cultivated by the early Romans a hundred years before Christ. Two hundred years later, Pliny, the Roman natural historian, detailed forty ancient varieties, all unknown today. He advised that "pears are harmful to eat raw, but good boiled with honey."

Pear trees in the Middle Ages flourished in castles, villas, and monastery gardens in the warm Mediterranean climates of Italy and France. For noblemen, a large orchard with exotic fruits was not only an adjunct of power, but a necessary expression of it. Pears were a favorite luxury. France imported them from Italy and gave them the French names many are known by today. According to court accounts, Britain imported dessert pears from France

Detail from "Still Life: Fruit, Bird, and Dwarf Pear Tree" by Charles V. Bond, 1856

during the reign of Henry III (1207–72). Britain's native pear (*Pyrus nivalis*, meaning "snow fruit") was hard and bitter, but was used to make an alcoholic cider called perry. Colorful old British names for their perry pears include the Wild Hedge Pear, the Lowsie Wild, the Crow Pear, and the Great Choke. The harsh, bitter, choking taste of British pears was said to be preferable to the French dessert pears, which made a "thin tasteless perry." The English herbalist Parkinson noted in 1629 that "the perry made of Choke Pears, not withstanding the harshness and evill taste, both of the fruit and juice, after a few months, becomes as milde and pleasante as wine."

For centuries, monks in cloistered monastery gardens developed the premium French and Italian dessert pears known for their delicious winelike flavor and smooth, melting texture. Each seedling could mean a wait of up to twenty years for the result, yet generations of patient monks developed hundreds of fine varieties, especially during the Renaissance. In Tuscany, one of the Medici grand dukes, Cosimo II, was said to have had 209 different varieties of pear served at his tables.

Exquisite yet fragile pears spread quickly throughout Europe and eventually to the New World. A European technique, still preferred today, of grafting a pear onto quince root stock, dwarfed the trees, bringing them to fruition sooner. The White Doyenné, a favorite in today's collections, was known to the Romans as Sementhinium and first imported to the New World from Italy in 1559.

The Rousselet de Reims was a favorite pear of King Louis XIV. La Quintinye, creator of the king's royal gardens at Versailles, claimed no garden should be without it. La Quintinye, like his king, loved pears. He wrote prolifically about the fruit and grew pears weighing as much as a kilo. His recorded list of a hundred pears, with their singsong French names, reads like a nursery rhyme. The best, he wrote, were the Bergamotte or Martin-sect, the Louise Bonne, and the Doyenné d'Automne, a smaller prototype of today's supermarket Comice. These great dessert pears were luxuries of nobility and wealth and not available to the common man.

In the eighteenth century, the Belgians took the lead from the French in developing new pear varieties. A priest at Mons, Nicolas Hardenpont, developed delicious Beurré (butter) varieties known for their juice and flavor. His work influenced Dr. Van Mons of Louvain to

The ancient Rousselet de Reims, a favorite of King Louis XIV

PEAR MYTHOLOGY

*I*n Greek mythology, *pear trees were sacred to Hera, whose statues were often made from their wood.*

Pear wood, *which gives off a pleasant odor when burned, was used in Pagan times in the Balkan region and eastern Europe as kindling for sacred fires for crop magic and to ensure the health of animals.*

The Circassians of southern Russia *regarded the pear tree as a protector of cattle. In autumn, on the day of the harvest festival, every household cut down a young pear tree in the forest and took it indoors with great ceremony. The trees were decorated with candles and topped with cheese. After much merriment, which the cattle must have appreciated, the trees were put in the courtyard, where they remained for the year.*

Birth Trees *are a European custom where an apple tree is planted for the birth of a boy and a pear tree for a girl. The trees are blessed, often at the time of the child's baptism. In some cultures the spirit of the tree is believed to protect the child's soul and mirror their growth.*

develop an amazing 400 pears, including the Beurré d'Anjou, our green supermarket Anjou pear, and the cinnamon colored Beurré Bosc, which today goes by Bosc only. By the mid-1800s, the Royal Horticultural Society in England counted 627 varieties growing in their gardens at Chiswick, including the popular Doyenné du Comice (Comice).

Pear cuttings were brought from Europe to the American colonies. Pioneers used the fruit for eating and baking, the fine-grained wood for making furniture, and even the leaves to make a rich yellow dye. Perry, an alcoholic drink made from pears, was popular, but not as common as cider. Until pear growing was established on the West Coast, a good pear, imitating European standards, was a luxury of the leisure class and not a commonly disseminated fruit like the apple, peach, or cherry. Though treated royally in Europe, New World pears could not compete with America's favorite fruit, the apple. Johnny Appleseed became a part of our heritage, but the pear had no legendary counterpart, partly because pear trees grown from seed rarely produce usable fruit, but rather small rocklike fruits resembling wild pears. In addition, the pear tree preferred a milder climate and did not grow well in the climatic extremes of the East Coast, with its prolonged freezing and hot, humid temperatures.

By the mid-nineteenth century, the fireblight disease was introduced in North America, most likely from imported Asian ornamentals. This disease devastated East Coast orchards. The only pear not affected was the barely palatable Kieffer pear, which is a hybrid of European and blight-resistant Asian species.

No occupation is so delightful to me as the cultivation of the earth.

—THOMAS JEFFERSON

THOMAS JEFFERSON AND THE PEARS OF MONTICELLO

As well as being America's first distinguished viticulturist, or wine grower, Thomas Jefferson was a noted connoisseur and grower of fine fruit. Fruit growing engaged what Jefferson called his "natural inclinations." His eight-acre fruit garden, which he called "the fruitery," included a 400-tree south orchard, a gentleman's fruit garden in the Old World horticultural tradition.

Between 1769 and 1814, he planted over 1,000 pear, apple, cherry, plum apricot, and quince trees, and he also experimented with perfecting his varieties. Even though Jefferson's orchards were fenced in, travelers commonly helped themselves to the harvest, as was common practice.

In his north orchard, called the farm or field orchard, Jefferson grew lesser fruit harvested for cider, brandy, and livestock feed. In The Fruits and Fruit Trees of Monticello (*University Press of Virginia, 1998*), author Peter Hatch says "there is some truth to one historian's tongue-and-cheek remark that it was a significant event when Americans began eating their fruit rather than drinking it." The fruitery at Monticello was unique because it was both an Old World fruit garden and a colonial farm orchard.

Thomas Jefferson had lived in Paris as the American minister to France and grew to love European pears. He planted seventeen European varieties at Monticello. Though he contracted specialists, including his Scottish gardener, Robert Bailey, to graft dessert pear varieties, he found them difficult to grow in Virginia's warm, humid climate. In a letter from Paris, Jefferson wrote that European pears were not simply "better than ours" but "infinitely beyond anything we possess." One notable exception was the Seckel. When Thomas Jefferson tasted the little red and gold pears from Philadelphia, he claimed "they exceed anything I have tasted since I left France."

Jefferson also planted the Old World Crassane, Beurré Gris, and St. Germaine pears. In 1981, Monticello began a restoration of the south orchard to preserve the historical landscaping of Jefferson's day and the fine pear varieties Jefferson loved. Monticello is open to the public and offers tours and fruit tastings (see page 154).

West Coast pears have their own unique history. They were originally brought by the Spanish to Mexico, Peru, and Chile, and traveled up the California coast with the early missions. Like the mild Mediterranean region, California has coastal valleys that are hot and dry in the summer and cold but not freezing in winter, perfect conditions for pears. The early mission settlers brought only what was essential, but that included pear budwood. They were carefully wrapped in wet straw or mud packs and packed in covered wagons or on the back of a mule to make the long journey up the California coast, where the budwood could be grafted onto quince.

The boom in California pear growing came after the Gold Rush, in the late 1800s, when farmers

planted large orchards of European pears to provide fruits for a growing population. Markets remained local and townsfolk enjoyed fresh fruit up until World War II. After the war, the small, easily bruised heritage varieties were gradually eliminated in favor of a large pear that could be shipped, handled, and had a long shelf life: namely the Bartlett. The inland coastal valleys of California, Oregon, and Washington became the largest pear growing area in the United States, growing 90 percent of the pear crop, mostly Bartletts. In the 1950s, the pear pack was destined for fruit cocktail and other syrupy can fillers, but today's processed pears are more likely to end up as the base for a health juice, a flavored wine, or baby food.

THE

Gentleman's Recreation:

OR THE

SECOND PART

OF THE

ART of GARDENING

IMPROVED.

Containing several New EXPERIMENTS and Curious OBSERVATIONS relating to FRUIT-TREES:

Particularly, a New METHOD of building Walls with *Horizontal Shelters.*

Illustrated with Copper Plates.

-----*Si quid novisti rectius istis,*
Candidus imperti; si non, his utere mecum.　　Hor.

By JOHN LAWRENCE, M. A. Rector of *Yelvertoft* in *Northamptonshire.*

To which is added by way of APPENDIX, A new and familiar way to find a most exact Meridian Line by the Pole-Star: whereby Gentlemen may know the true Bearings of their Houses and Garden-Walls, and regulate their Clocks and Watches, &c. By *Edward Lawrence,* Brother to the Author of this Book.

The SECOND EDITION.

LONDON: Printed for BERNARD LINTOTT between the *Temple-Gates* in *Fleetstreet.* 1717.

According to The Gentleman's Recreation, *by John Lawrence, 1716, "The design of [this] treatise is to put Gentlemen into a Method of having the most and the best of all sorts of fruit, and that in the easiest, the cheapest and most expeditious ways."*

THE LOST ORCHARDS OF THE CALIFORNIA MISSIONS

*L*egends of the early California missions claim that Father Junipero Serra planted pear seeds at each mission as he traveled north up the state. Though Father Serra did not actually plant pear trees himself, one of his surviving letters, dated 1777 (eight years after he arrived in California), speaks of improvements needed, including "grafts from fruit trees . . . and grapevines." Two years later, grape vines were reported at the missions, and fruit probably arrived also. The early Spanish fathers were required to record annual *informes* for grain and livestock production, but not for fruit and vegetables, so letters written by the fathers, visitors, and traders are the only remaining records.

The visiting French naturalist La Pérouse brought pear scions for grafting to the missions, along with other fruit, in 1786. Six years later, a visiting Englishman, George Vancouver, was amazed at the Mission San Buenaventura garden. He wrote, "Apples, pears, plums, figs, oranges, peaches and pomegranates . . . all these were flourishing in the greatest health and perfection though separated from the seaside by only two or three fields of corn." The padres found instructions for grafting and other horticultural tasks in the Spanish text *Agricultura General*, which included instructions on soil content, proper location, and such details as whether various tasks should be performed in the full of the moon or the crescent.

By 1828, Mission San Buenaventura was reported to have ten orchards of fruit trees. At Mission San Gabriel, an 1834 inventory counts nine orchards with a total of 2,333 trees. One imagines that these abundant orchards, with their great diversity of fruit spreading

Mission San Juan Bautista is the site of the oldest pear tree in California. The tree, planted in 1810, has survived in spite of generations of neglect and is still producing. Father Ed Fitz-Henry of Mission San Juan Bautista counted exactly twenty-one pears on the tree last fall, which is remarkable, as he noted, because California has exactly twenty-one missions. The tree is shown below with botanical artist (and this book's calligrapher) Wayne David Hand.

farther than the eye can see, must have been as much a monument to the faith as the mission architecture.

Native American laborers cared for the trees. They carried gourds full of water from the closest stream, one gourdful for each tree. When the fruit was ripe, the Indians gathered the crop in large baskets and carried it to the mission, where it was sorted and stored. Pears of good keeping quality were stored until spring on shelves covered with a thick layer of straw, in buildings with walls made of thick, cool adobe. Some of the fruit was cut and dried on a flat roof and used as a snack or in salsas. In Spanish tradition, fresh fruit was preserved in jams, jellies, and delectable fruit candies.

In the dry, grassy fields surrounding mission grounds, very little remains of the old mission orchards today except an occasional walnut tree or a gnarled twisted pear still bearing an odd-shaped fruit.

The daughter of Don José Jesus Vallejo, a Mission San José administrator, looks back on the mission gardens she remembers:

> They were, I think, more extensive and contained a greater variety of trees and plants than most people can imagine. . . . I remember that at Mission San José we had many varieties of seedling fruits which have now been lost to cultivation. Of pears we had four sorts, one ripening in early summer, one in late summer, and two in autumn and winter. The Spanish names of these pears were the Presidenta, the Bergamota, the Pana and the Lechera. One of them was as large as a Bartlett, but there are no trees left of it now.

> —FROM *INDIAN LIFE AT THE OLD MISSIONS*, BY EDITH BUCKLAND WEBB

PEAR TREES, LIVING ARCHITECTURE IN THE GOLDEN AGE

*I*n the early 1900s, industrial monarchs like Rockefeller, Vanderbilt, and Hearst made huge fortunes in America on assembly-line technology, and then spent them on lavish estates that served as monuments to themselves. Modeled on classical European design, the estates included elaborate gardens and abundant orchards that boasted of wealth and self-sufficiency. The orchard was a refined gentleman's hobby. Superior fruit not only charmed his dinner guests but would win recognition in horticultural society competitions. In the golden age of gardening, a gentleman's status was enhanced by the size and taste of his produce.

The estate fruit collection was well managed by the gardener, who trained at the finest European schools of horticulture and apprenticed under a head estate gardener. These gardeners knew when to pick a Louise Bonne and how to properly chill and ripen the White Doyenné.

"The garden is but a prolongation of the house," claimed Edith

Double-U espaliers of Louise Bonne d'Arranches from The Lorette System of Pruning, *1925*

Wharton, the blueblood novelist of the 1920s. Her classic book *Italian Villas and Their Gardens* was a how-to guide for the rich, illustrated by no less a talent than Maxfield Parrish. Fruit variety was an important part of the classic Italian garden, not only in the orchard but in the formal gardens.

Like the main house, the classic formal garden was divided by hedges or walls into compartments, or garden rooms, each with its own distinct character: sunny fruit trees in one room, another a cool mossy grotto, still another with reflective pools and marble Greek

ASIAN PEAR HISTORY

*I*n China, Asian pears are called Li, and in Japan, Nashi. They are considered exotic in the West for their unique sweet taste and crunchy texture, but in China the Asian pear is as popular as the apple is in the United States. A hotel guest in China will likely find an Asian pear left on the pillow as an evening dessert.

Asian pears have been bred since ancient times, but are not common to all of Asia, only China, Korea, and Japan. Dr. Wang Yulin, a pear breeder from the Hunan province of China, says books referring to the Chinese pear were written as early as 1134 B.C. In The Shiji, a Chinese book from around 93 B.C., the Zengdin Yuli variety is described as "large as a fist, sweet as honey, and crisp as a water chestnut." Grafting methods for the Chinese pear can be found dating back for more than 1,000 years. In his book Chinese Pears, Dr. Yulin describes thirty-four varieties now grown in China.

The Asian pears grown in the northwestern United States are of Japanese or Korean origin. With their growing popularity and the new varieties being developed, Asian pear production is expanding worldwide, to the United States, New Zealand, Australia, Argentina, Chile, and France. Thirty-six varieties are available through mail-order nurseries in the United States. (See page 152.)

Willow-leaved pear, a decorative variety illustrated by Wayne David Hand.

gods. Pear trees neatly espaliered on the garden stucco walls created not only a sense of abundancy, but order. Curiously, flowers were of secondary importance. Primary in the classic garden was serenity and quiet, diversity with repose. The shapes of the espalied pear and the neatly pruned courtyard trees exemplified a harmonious living architecture, serving the garden architects' ideal of adapting nature without distorting it.

> It's to the glory of the Italian architects that neglect and disintegration cannot wholly mar the effects they were skilled in creating: effects due to such a fine sense of proportion, to so exquisite a perception of the relation between architecture and landscape, between verdure and marble, that while a trace of their plan remains one feels the spell of the whole.
>
> —EDITH WHARTON
> *ITALLIAN VILLAS AND THEIR GARDENS*

Filoli:
An Early
California
Estate

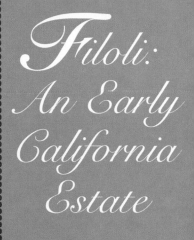

The Filoli estate in Woodside,
California, has a 36,000-
square-foot main house with
forty-three rooms, sixteen acres
of formal gardens, and a ten-acre
mixed-fruit orchard.

FILOLI'S EARLY TWENTIETH CENTURY ESTATE ORCHARD

William Bowers Bourn II, educated at Cambridge, exemplified the wealthy class in Northern California. He managed the Empire Mine, the largest and richest gold mine operating in California in the late 1800s, and later built the Greystone Winery, known today as Christian Brothers. In the aftermath of the 1906 earthquake, Bourn, like many other San Francisco residents, relocated to a rural area. He purchased the Spring Valley Water Company in 1908, known today as the San Francisco Water Department, and bought land adjacent to the company's watershed, in a coastal valley thirty miles south of San Francisco, for his country estate. He named his estate Filoli, which is a contraction of the first two letters of the words *fight*, *love*, and *live*, from Bourn's credo, "To fight for a just cause, to love your fellow man, to live a good life."

A 36,000-square-foot residence of forty-three rooms was built, and sixteen acres of formal gardens were tastefully landscaped according to classical garden principals. The main axis of the formal gardens is a wide allée (walkway) of Irish yew trees, flanked on either side with espaliered apple and pear trees, parallel to the main house.

In 1919, Bourn planted a ten-acre mixed-fruit orchard. A thousand of the finest European and American varieties of pears, apples, plums, peaches, walnuts, and figs were planted in the valley east of the residence.

Beautiful Filoli represents the ideal oasis garden where one learns the classic rules of gardening.

—PENELOPE HOBHOUSE, WRITER AND GARDEN DESIGNER FOR QUEEN ELIZABETH (II)

Spring 1922: William Bowers Bourn II examines the flowers on the pear trees at his Filoli estate.

Filoli's coastal valley, with its warm, dry summers and cool winter temperatures, was perfect for growing pome fruits, the family that includes pears, apples, and quince. Bourn's head gardener, trained in Europe, knew the optimum times for picking, cold storage, and ripening each variety. Bourn's cook and butler knew to poach the Seckel, and serve the Doyenné fresh with a dollop of crème fraîche. Like today's privileged class who cultivate art collections, Bourn and the gentry of his time cultivated fine fruit collections not only for enjoyment but as a symbol of success.

Saving Heritage Pears at Filoli

A well-cared-for pear tree can live for hundreds of years. Even without care, pears have earned a reputation for being great survivors. It is the pear tree, above all other fruits, including apples, apricots, plums, peaches, figs, and walnuts, that survived forty years of drought, deer and rodent predation, and neglect in the Filoli orchard. Originally ten acres, the orchard was planted in 1919 with 1,000 trees spaced twenty feet apart. Today, only 150 trees remain, 50 of them pears. Three trees recently identified as Dearborn (1818), an American seedling, may be the only trees of their kind still in existence. Other survivors include the russeted Conference (1885), a winter pear from England that resembles a small brown gourd; Duchesse d'Angoulême (1808), a squat, knobby, French pear known for its melting, buttery flesh and delicious flavor; and Jargonelle (1629), thought to have been grown by the ancient Romans. Many Filoli pears remain unidentified, a wealth of germplasm (genetic material) and history yet to be discovered.

When Mrs. William P. Roth, the second owner of the estate, graciously deeded Filoli to the National Trust for Historic Preservation in 1976, staffing and resources were limited. Preservation maintenance was focused on the formal gardens and historic buildings, leaving the orchard unattended. Lucy Tolmach, director of horticulture at Filoli since 1972, sees the orchard as "one of the character-defining features of the American country place. The continuing decline of the Filoli orchard represented a serious loss of integrity for the historic landscape and a permanent loss of germ plasm." With her horticultural staff and C. Todd Kennedy, a member of

Dearborn pear (above). The Filoli Estate (right), circa 1928. A ten-year-old orchard of a thousand mixed fruit trees is shown in a boot shape (left of the main house). Two hundred fifty additional fruit trees were planted in the panel garden (above the house) and espaliered along the formal garden walls.

California Rare Fruit Growers, Inc., she developed a strategy for preserving the orchard: "The first step was to document and identify the fruit trees and to begin a propagation program to preserve the remaining authentic germ plasm. The second step, when funds became available, was to stabilize and protect the remaining trees and rehabilitate the orchard."

Todd Kennedy, one of California's leading fruit preservationists and historians, has collected fruit by taking budwood from derelict orchards all over the country, especially in New England. He also receives wood from state agricultural stations phasing out their collections. His private collection has grown to include 2,500 fruit trees, including varieties of rare old French and Italian dessert pears, some on the verge of extinction.

In the fall of 1997, the Filoli governing board approved the orchard rehabilitation project, which included accepting 200 fruit trees, including sixty recently budded pear trees from Todd Kennedy. Filoli will preserve the orchard and replant it with varieties from the periods of its previous owners. Many endangered fruit varieties have found a permanent home on this historic estate. With the addition of Mr. Kennedy's trees, the Filoli collection of pome fruit will be the largest in private hands in North America.

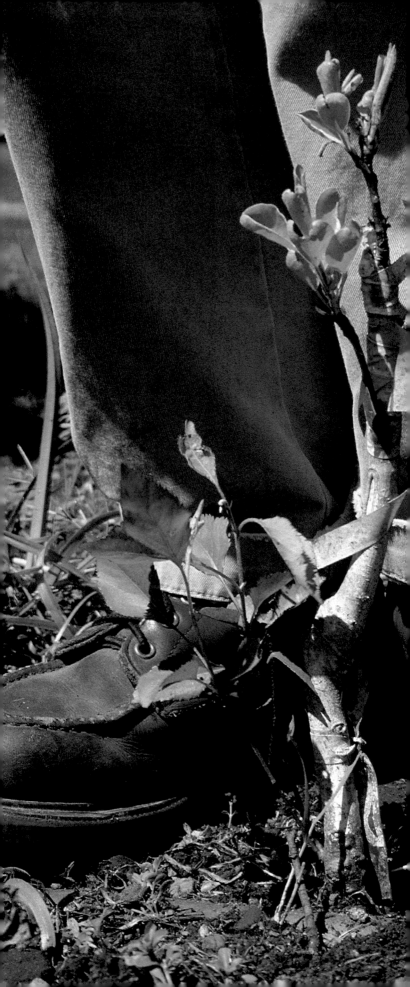

Pears
in the
Garden

May I never miss a rainbow or a sunset because I am looking down.

—SOURCE UNKNOWN

GROWING AND HARVESTING PEARS IN THE HOME GARDEN

Lucy Tolmach

Filoli Estate, Director of Horticulture

What are some basic requirements for growing good pears?

Pears require full sun at least 8 hours per day and reasonable drainage. They can withstand some flooding, especially in the winter, and are quite drought-tolerant when established. Depending on the variety, they all require winter chilling in order to produce fruit. European pears require between 900 and 1,200 hours of chilling below 45 degrees. Asian pears require only 600 hours of chilling. Pear blossoms and young fruit can be damaged at temperatures approaching 32 degrees and below. Most varieties need a compatible variety for cross-pollination for good production. Climates with warm, humid conditions are not good for pears because such climates favor fire blight. Pears thrive in places with low humidity, bright sunshine, and a moderate, cool growing season, like the West Coast.

How do I begin caring for a new pear tree?

Purchase your new pear as a branched tree or unbranched "whip" ($1/2$- to $3/4$-inch size) from a mail-order nursery specializing in fruit. They will ship at the appropriate time for planting in your climate zone. Keep the roots moist until planted. The soil should not be wet when the hole is dug. Dig the hole large enough to accommodate the root system comfortably without having to cut or twist any roots. If your tree is a dwarf, place the junction where the tree is grafted 2 inches above the soil level. Do not use any amendment or fertilizer in the hole. It can burn new roots. Slowly refill the hole with soil, using the end of the

Notched or T-shaped wooden boughs can be propped under a pear tree's branches to help support the weight of the fruit.

> *In the Spring at the end of the day,*
> *you should smell like dirt.*
>
> —Margaret Atwood

shovel handle to work the soil gently around the roots. Water thoroughly when the hole is half filled with soil and, when this drains down, continue filling. When finished, raise the sides of the hole to form a basin to hold water around the tree, and water deeply. Remove the basin during periods of heavy rainfall, to avoid flooding.

Once the tree has been planted, cut it back to a point 24 to 30 inches from the ground, making the pruning cut $1/4$ inch above a good, healthy bud. Remove any side branches back to the main trunk. Exposed wood can overheat in the sun, so paint the trunk with white latex paint to prevent sunburn.

How do I train my new tree?

In the spring, after planting and heading back, watch the new buds as they sprout and grow. When they are 8 to 10 inches long, select a maximum of 4 branches. The top branch will assume the role of the leader. Choose well-spaced branches with wide angles of attachment, because these will be stronger. Be careful not to select any branches from below the bud or graft union. Remove all other branches at the main trunk. Make sure you keep a close watch on your tree, rubbing off any other buds that sprout from the trunk through the rest of the growing season. In a couple of years, once the main framework has been established and the tree has reached a height of about 6 to 8 feet, the central leader should be cut just above an upper side branch, called a modified leader, which will help to reduce further upward growth of the tree. Restrict any additional pruning to removal of unwanted vertical sprouts from the trunk or the rootstock, weak or crisscrossing growth, or diseased branches. Heavy pruning will delay bearing.

What are the watering requirements for pears?

Newly planted pears need to be deep watered at least every 2 weeks, depending on the weather and the soil conditions. Established trees are extremely drought-tolerant, but they bear more fruit if they are deep watered at least monthly through the growing season.

How about fertilizing requirements?

Pears have low fertilizer requirements. Avoid high nitrogen fertilization in the spring because it will encourage new growth, which is very susceptible to fire blight and pear scab. If you need nitrogen, fertilize in the fall..

How can I control weeds?

Keep weeds from growing around the new tree by hand weeding or using mulch. New trees will not establish if they are competing with weeds, and rodents who live in tall grasses are more likely to girdle trees.

Can pears be grown well in containers?

Dwarf pears on quince rootstock can be grown in 24-by-24-inch (or larger) containers, but they will require staking, repotting every year during the dormant season, regular water, and fertilizer.

Is it necessary to stake my pear?

Dwarf trees need staking because they bear more fruit than standards and are usually shallow-rooted. Standard and midsize trees do not require staking.

Can I espalier any pear tree?

Choose a dwarf European pear that has been budded on quince rootstock because it will grow slower and is easier to train. All European varieties are spur bearing (versus tip bearing), meaning they produce fruit along the full length of their branches. The pear, with graceful leaves and knarled wood, is the classic espalier used on the grounds of Versailles, but it is also perfect along a sunny wall in the small garden. *(See photo pg. 15)*

STEP-BY-STEP BUDDING TECHNIQUE

Pear trees offered in garden centers and grown in commercial orchards are produced in the same manner, a specialized form of grafting called budding. When budding, the wholesale nursery worker cuts out a single bud from a branch of the tree he or she wishes to propagate and inserts it into the thin stem of a rootstock, usually a seedling, intended to be "worked over," or grafted, to the new variety. This technique is a very economical use of propagating material and is accomplished in the late summer and fall after the buds become dormant. A shoot from the current season's growth at leats 1/4 inch in diameter contain-ing well-developed buds is selected as a bud source. The leaves are removed. Large buds from the lower part of the stick are preferred. To propagate pear trees, one must order rootstocks the preceding winter from mail-order nurseries (see page 155). The rootstocks are then planted out in a nursery row. In late summer and fall the leaves are removed from the lower 6" of the rootstock, which should be at least 3/8" in diameter.

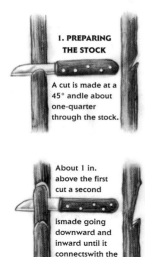

1. PREPARING THE STOCK

A cut is made at a 45° andle about one-quarter through the stock.

About 1 in. above the first cut a second

ismade going downward and inward until it connectswith the first cut.

1. *Using a razor-sharp knife, remove a shal-low wedge of bark about 1 inch long x 1/2 inch wide from a straight section of the root-stock stem approximately 1 to 2 inches from the ground, on the north side of the rootstock. Make the first cut at a 45°angle about one-quarter through the stock. At about 1 inch above the first cut, make a cut in a wedge shape downward until it intersects with the first cut. The shape of the wedge that is removed should match the shape of the bud to be inserted so that the inserted bud will fit like a piece in a puzzle.*

2.PREPARING THE BUD
The cuts remov-ing the bud from the bud stick are made just as those

in the stock. The lower cut is made about 1/4 in. below the bud.

2. *To prepare the bud, grasp the bud stick firmly and, starting at the bottom bud, make the first cut on a 45°angle 1/4 inch below the bud about one-quarter through the stock. Make a second cut about 1/2 inch above the bud ina downward motion, connecting with the first cut. A superficial slice at the bot-tom cut will disconnect the bud from the bud stick.*

A second cut is made about 1/2 in. above the

bud, coming downward behind the bud and connecting with the first cut, permitting there-moval of the bud piece.

Inserting the bud into the stock

3. *Insert the bud by lifting the newly cut bud off the bud stick and insert it into the rootstock, making sure that the bud is facing up (as it was on the bud stick).*

Appearance of bud and stock ready to be placed together.

4. *Bind the wound with a length of budding tape, which is tucked under itself to hold the bud in place. The wound can also be painted with a latex grafting seal to prevent desiccation.*

The chips bud is finally wrapped.

Aftercare

The bud will take several months to heal, but won't start to grow until the following spring. The rootstock should be partially cut off in early spring to force the inserted bud to break and completely removed 2 weeks after the bud is actively growing. Throughout the first growing season, constant attention must be paid to ensure that buds from the rootstock don't break from below and overtake the inserted bud. The budding tape must be carefully removed after the bud has taken and before it constricts

the young tree. By the end of the season, you will have a young pear tree. If the season has been long and warm, the tree may be ready to dig and plant into its permanent location, or it may be left in the nursery row to add a further season's growth before it is transplanted.

The grafted bud wrapped in budding tape.

PICKING AND STORING

When do you harvest pears?

European pears, like avocados, should be harvested when they are green and firm, and should not be tree ripened. If you leave pears on a tree until they turn yellow and start falling on the ground, they will be mushy and flavorless. Harvest dates will vary according to your climate zone. The number of days from bloom to harvest is fairly standard for each variety, ranging from 105 to 190 days. Harvest pears later in cool years and earlier in warm years. Observe any changes in the color and size of the fruit. When the dots on the skin, called *lenticels*, start to become conspicuous and contrast with the color of the skin, it means harvest time is nearing. Cut a pear open to check the color of the seeds. Light-colored seeds mean immature fruit. Dark brown seeds mean the pear is ready for harvesting. An easy test for readiness is to gently cradle a pear in the palm of your hand and then lift it slowly so that the stem is perpendicular to the spur that it is attached to. If the pear is ready for harvesting, it will come off in your hand without any resistance. Pears picked too soon will shrivel. Pears picked too late will be mushy and without good flavor. Summer pears, like Clapp's Favorite, are ready for harvesting in late July, and winter pears, like Winter Nélis, are not ready until October and November. Asian pears are ripened on the tree between August and October. Look for color changes and taste the fruit for sweetness. They ripen unevenly, requiring several pickings.

What is the proper way to pick a pear?

All pears bruise easily. Hold the spur, or fruiting branch, in one hand to avoid damaging it. With your other hand, lift and twist the pear off the spur, stem and all. Do not pull straight down. If the pear resists, it is not ready to be picked. Carefully place each pear into a picking bag, which is a cloth or nylon bag with a large strap that goes over your head and across your chest. Do not drop the fruits or handle the bags roughly. Three-legged orchard ladders are designed for safe use on uneven ground and are needed for harvesting trees, hedgerows, and espaliered trees. Don't load the bag more than halfway. It can damage the fruit and cause instability on the ladder. Some varieties, like Bartlett, are picked twice, because not all pears on a tree will be ready at the same time.

How do I handle, store, and ripen homegrown pears?

After picking, place the pears gently into shallow cardboard, plastic, or wooden boxes, one layer deep, with the stem up. Most European pears benefit from a period in cold storage, which improves their flavor, texture, and fragrance. A refrigerator set between 34 and 40 degrees works well, as long as there is plenty of room for good air circulation. Open the door periodically to release excess ethylene gas, which can scald the pears. Pears should be kept in cold storage for at least 4 weeks, depending on the variety. Pears are removed from cold storage, for ripening, and put into a cool (about 60 to 65 degrees), dark place. Some varieties take 5 days to ripen; others take as long as 14 days. Check the fruits daily to observe changes in color, fragrance, and firmness. Asian pears store well through winter, but Shinseiki and Twentieth Century lose their acidity and the charm of their flavor under refrigeration.

PROBLEMS WITH PEARS

My pear tree did not produce any pears this year. Why?

If you live in a mountainous area or the colder regions of the United States, your pear blossoms might have been damaged by cold winter or early spring temperatures (32 degrees or lower). If you live in a warmer area of the country, especially the South, Southeast, or Southwest, your climate may be too warm to produce enough chilling hours below 45 degrees, which are required to break dormancy. Select varieties that are adapted to your specific climate zone. Mail-order nursery catalogs are your best source of information for selecting the right variety. See page 155.

Pears may not bear fruit for several other reasons. It may take 7 to 10 years for a standard pear to bear fruit. Dwarf trees usually take somewhere between 3 to 5 years to bear.

Pears usually need another variety for cross-pollination. Nursery catalogs are the best source for selecting a variety to pollinate your tree.

Pears require honeybees, flies, and other insects for pollination. If it is cold (55 degrees or lower) and rainy when the pears are in bloom, these pollinators will not be able to fly.

Also, pear trees, especially Asian pears, are somewhat biennial in bearing, which means they may produce a heavy crop one year and fewer the following year.

My new pear tree has been girdled at the base of the trunk. What can I do?

Meadow mice, moles, and rabbits will chew on the trunks of young and mature pear trees. Keep weeds and tall grasses away from the tree trunks, especially during the winter when other food sources are scarce. Protect the trunks of newly planted trees with plastic rodent guards or circular wire cages.

At the base of my tree there are suckers coming up with foliage that look different from the ones growing on the rest of the tree. What are they?

Pears are propagated by grafting or budding onto rootstock. What you are seeing are suckers coming up from the rootstock. This sometimes happens when the rootstock is more vigorous than the scion, or when the bud or graft union is placed too high. Prune (or even better, yank) these suckers off where they originate, or they will overtake the main trunk in time.

My pear tree produces so much fruit that the limbs break. Any suggestions?

If a tree bears a lot of fruit, it should be thinned in late May or June, or when fruit are about the size of a golf ball. With your fingers, gently remove small, weak, or misshapen fruit, thinning out crowded fruits and leaving one or two fruits per cluster. The remaining pears will be larger, sweeter, less prone to disease, and showier, with a nicer color.

Asian pears are known for their heavy bearing and need to be thinned twice during the season, right after the bloom when the fruit has set and again when the fruit reaches golf-ball size.

This spring, several branches on my pear tree wilted and turned black. They look like they were torched.

Your tree probably has a bacterial disease called *fire blight*. Honeybees spread this disease as they pollinate the flowers in the spring. Rainy, warm, spring weather will aggravate the problem. Fire blight, an American disease, is a real problem in many areas. It is the single most important reason why pears have not been more widely cultivated in North America. To deal with fire blight, prune out infected branches and burn the prunings. Make sure you disinfect your pruning tools with rubbing alcohol after each cut, to avoid spreading the disease from branch to branch. Plant disease-resistant varieties if you live in an area where fire blight is a problem. Avoid heavy nitrogen fertilization in the spring and heavy pruning that will encourage new growth. New growth is very susceptible to the disease.

The Pear
Collection

EUROPEAN AND AMERICAN PEARS

PYRUS COMMUNIS

DESCRIPTIONS BY C.T. KENNEDY

*T*odd Kennedy, well recognized as one of California's leading fruit preservationists and historians, is descended from an old family of Santa Clara fruit growers and is dedicated to the preservation of heritage varieties. An attorney, Mr. Kennedy's avocation and true passion is collecting fruit by taking budwood from derelict orchards all over the country, especially in the many remaining in New England. He also receives wood from state agricultural stations phasing out their collections. His collection has grown to include 2,500 fruit trees, including varieties of rare old French and Italian dessert pears, some on the verge of extinction.

IDENTIFICATION GLOSSARY

• **BLUSH:** Skin pigmentation; a solid rose, coral, or brownish red cheek marking, appearing only on the sunny side of the fruit.

• **LENTICELS:** Pores that appear as spots of coloration on the skin when a pear is ripe; the contrasting color of the lenticels against thin background is an indication of ripeness. *Example: Forelle (red lenticels)*

• **LI:** Generic name for Chinese Asian pears.

• **MATURE:** Fruit that readily separates from the tree and has seed capable of germination. Fruit may be physiologically mature but not yet ripe.

• **NASHI:** Generic name for Japanese Asian pears.

• **PERRY:** The fermented juice of bitter pears common to England, comparable to apple cider. *Example: Petit Muscat*

• **POME FRUITS:** The family that includes pears, apples and quince.

• **RIPE:** A subjective standard of taste describing the taste and texture of fruit. Palatability. A mature fruit becomes ripe when it is pleasing to eat.

• **RUSSETED:** Red to yellow brown mottling on skin. *Example: Conference, Duchesse d'Angoulême, Bosc (fully russeted)*

• **SUMMER PEAR:** A pear harvested July through August. Some summer pears can be eaten from the tree without a period of cold storage. *Example: Bartlett, Clapp's Favorite, Jargonelle*

• **WINTER PEAR:** Harvested October through December. Winter pears usually have thicker skin and more grit, and require a cold storage period. *Example: Winter Nélis, Passe Crassanne*

(Tasting Glossary on Pages 86-87)

Abbé Fetel
(ah-BEY fey-TAHL)
FRANCE, 1869

During the winter months, this unusually shaped pear is found in European markets. Its name commemorates a parish vicar (an abbot named Fetel) in the South of France, who found this as a seedling in 1869. In Italy, where the variety is grown exclusively, it is known as Abate. Rather dry, especially towards the end of its market period, Abbé mellows to a slightly sharp, fine-textured fruit.

Amiré Joannet
(SEE JARGONELLE)

HOW BARTLETT GOT ITS NAME

In the late eighteenth century, a British schoolmaster named Stair discovered the seedling in Berkshire, England. It was popularized by a nurseryman named Williams, who fancied it resembled the ancient variety Bon Chrétien. Thomas Brewer had the pear imported for his estate in Massachusetts. After Enoch Bartlett purchased the estate in 1817, he distributed the pear under his own name, Bartlett. Today Bartlett is the most widely grown pear in the world and accounts for 70 percent of all United States commercial plantings.

Bartlett

ENGLAND, 1700

This most popular of pears is known to the rest of the world as Williams' Bon Chrétien, or just Williams. One of the larger pears, it is harvested while green in late July or early August in the Pacific Coast states. When ripened to bright yellow, Bartlett's flesh is very juicy, with a sweet, buttery, musky flavor. If left on the tree to ripen, it will decay rapidly.

Red Bartlett
UNITED STATES, 1934

This natural red mutation of the Bartlett,
is identical to the regular Bartlett, with the same
juiciness and melting flesh as Bartlett,
as well as the same characteristic musky
aroma. In commerce, the Red Bartlett
is too often stored far beyond its
prime. Like Bartlett, it is a
summer pear and it
should never see the
October page of
the calendar.

Belle Lucrative
(BEL lu-cra-TEEV)
(*not pictured*) BELGIUM, 1831
(ALSO CALLED FONDANTE D'AUTOMNE,
ESPÉRENS HERRENBIRNE)

Truly one of the great autumn pears, Belle
Lucrative is unfortunately rarely encountered. Better
known in Britain than the United States, this
variety is attributed to Major Espéren's nursery in
Mechelen, Belgium. It is small, but outstanding for
its sweetness and acidity, a combination known to
fruit-lovers as "richness." It has a very fine-grained
texture and is juicy when well grown.

Bergamotte d'Été
(ber-ga-MAHT deh-teh)
ITALY, BEFORE 1600S

Typical of the class of pear called Bergamotte,
this pear is named after the city of Bergamo in
Italy, where it is said to have originated in the
sixteenth century. Bergamottes are smaller in size
than most pears, characteristically round in form,
and quite juicy, though rather sharp in flavor. The
Bergamotte d'Été (Summer Bergamotte) comes in
late July. The other Bergamottes are generally
autumn pears. Another unique feature is that all
vegetative parts of the Bergamotte d'Été tree grow
a fine woolen fluff covering. As with all summer
pears, the fruits are to be eaten as
soon as picked.

Bergamotte Espéren
(ber-ga-MAHT es-pair-EN)

BELGIUM, 1831

This is the finest variety left to us by Major Espéren, pear breeder of Mechelen, Belgium. It's an autumn-ripening Bergamotte, but unlike others of its class, this fruit stores well until the beginning of winter. Its thick, tough skin withstands the storage in cellars and barns that was typical in the days before refrigeration. Like most winter pears, its texture is rather coarse. The flavor is sharp, suggesting citrus. It is good for juice early in the season, and for cooking later on.

Beurré Bosc

BELGIUM, 1807

(ALSO CALLED KAISER ALEXANDER)

A staple of the American market, the Bosc is among the few russet-skinned pears available. Not difficult to grow, this variety is, however, a demanding pear to finish for the table, requiring both care in timing the moment of harvest and patience in waiting for the fruit to mellow into dessert condition. When harvested too soon, it becomes wooden and juiceless. For the best fruit, look for Boscs with decidedly yellow skin undertones. At its best, the Bosc has a melting, slightly fibrous flesh and a nutty flavor with hints of vanilla and spice. Saturated with syrupy juice, the Bosc has the highest sugar content of all commercial pears.

Buttira Precoce Morettini
(bu-TIR-ah pray-COACH-ay mor-et-TEEN-ee)
ITALY, 1956

A recently developed Italian pear known simply as BPM. It is probably the earliest pear of commercial quality, ripening a few days ahead of Clapp's. Occasionally planted in Pacific Northwest orchards to provide pollen for other varieties, it rarely appears in markets. BPM is sweet and juicy and does not keep long.

Cascade
(not pictured) OREGON, 1988

This hybrid of Comice and Red Bartlett was developed by the Oregon Agricultural Experiment Station in Medford. It has the texture, flavor, and juiciness of Comice, but the tartness of Bartlett.

Clapp's Favorite
UNITED STATES, EARLY 1800S

Clapp's was introduced to North
America by a Boston fruit farmer by that
name in the early nineteenth century. It has
occupied the early-summer market ever since, in
the United States and abroad. Clapp's
resembles Bartlett, and passes for it in the
trade. Rarely, if ever, is it sold as Clapp's.
You can distinguish it by its pointed, puckered
blossom end (Bartlett is flat-bottomed).
Clapp's lacks any suggestion of Bartlett's
characteristic musky flavor. The fruit is
best when used fresh.

Beurré Clairgeau
(beuh-RAY claire-GO)
FRANCE, 1848

Often confused with Bartlett, Beurré Clairgeau is bigger and is a week or two later in the season. The largest of the dessert pears, the Clairgeau was very popular in this country at the beginning of the century. It has thin skin, and juicier and coarser flesh than that of Bartlett, but lacks that variety's musky aroma.

Coscia
(CO-sha)
TUSCANY (ITALY), ANCIENT

Coscia is still produced in northern Italy for specialty markets. It is a summer pear, harvested before Bartlett, but is smaller and does not keep as well under cold storage. Coscia has a good flavor, sweeter and less tart than other summer pears. A characteristic open, star-shaped calyx (the former flower) remains at the end of the fruit.

Doyenné du Comice
(doy-ehn-NAY du co-MEES)

FRANCE, 1849

(ALSO CALLED COMICE, ROYAL RIVIERA)

The Doyenné, which takes its name from the French word for a female dean, is the world's most famous pear. It was popularized in this country as a trademarked gift fruit at Christmas time, outstanding for its delicacy of flesh and its copious juice. Though the flavor is not rich (sugar balanced with acid), there is enough sweetness to satisfy American tastes, and some sharpness for those from abroad. The name commemorates the Comice Horticole, an agricultural society in Angers, France, where the Doyenné du Comice originated in 1848. The tree is unusually susceptible to every pear disease, so it is grown only in the most favorable fruit-growing climates, like the Pacific Northwest. Comice is a popular mail-order pear for dessert baskets, sold under trademark names like Royal Riviera.

It's sad to grow old, but nice to ripen.

—Brigitte Bardot

Red Comice
UNITED STATES, 1988
(ALSO CALLED RED CRIMSON)

This is a pigmented mutation of the regular Comice, but like so many colored sports (mutations), it is inferior to its parent in eating quality. Red Comice, a recent American invention, was discovered in Medford, Oregon. It is only now being planted in quantity.

> *One of the worst mistakes you can make as a gardener is to think you're in charge.*
>
> —JANET GILLESPIE

Conference

ENGLAND, 1884

Conference is the definitive English pear, first produced by the Rivers nursery and still grown commercially in Britain and Italy. It is found in all European markets during winter. One of its recognizable characteristics is its elongated, narrow neck. The skin can be russeted, though most markets prefer fruits with even yellow coloring. The flavor is fairly rich, both sweet and slightly sharp, but it can be dry if the fruit is left in refrigerated storage too long.

Beurré d'Anjou
(beuh-RAY dahn-JOU)
(ALSO CALLED NEC PLUS MEURIS)
BELGIUM, 1820

After the Bartlett, the Beurré d'Anjou is the
most popular pear in the United States because
of its iron resistance to the hazards of commercial
storage. It will keep under controlled-atmosphere
refrigeration (CA storage) for up to six months.
Harvested at the end of September, it can still be
found in supermarkets the end of the following
spring. D'Anjou is named after the Anjou region
in France. Fruit connoisseurs consider the Anjou
mediocre for dessert use. It is not remarkable for
its sweetness, but it develops a lemony flavor,
always a little sharp, and its texture
is always smooth.

Red d'Anjou
UNITED STATES, 1956

*This variety is a spontaneous mutation discov-
ered as a branch on a tree in an orchard of
Beurré d'Anjou pears. It is less frequently
encountered than many other red-skin pears
because it doesn't share the long-keeping
virtues of its parent, the Anjou.
However, it is increasing in
cultivation and production.*

NAUMES: THE LARGEST PEAR GROWER IN THE WORLD

*W*hat about the big growers, who grow the Anjou, Bartlett, Comice, and Bosc pears that we see in the supermarket? Sue Naumes and her brother Mike own Naumes, a fruit company that grows, packs, and ships pears, and even has its own juicing operation. The Naumes grow pears in California, Washington, and in Oregon at their picturesque home in the Rogue River Valley. According to the *Wall Street Journal*, Naumes is the largest pear grower in the world. The title suggests corporate America, business suits, and an "I'll get back to you" attitude, but when I arrived in Medford, Oregon, Sue Naumes answered the phone. "C'mon over to the house," she invited. "If you're interested in old fruit labels, I got 'em."

"But it's Sunday," I said, not wanting to impose.

"No, no, come on over. If I'm working thirteen hours a day, six days a week anyway, what does it matter?" She sounded like my Wisconsin relatives.

"You work thirteen-hour days?"

"And I'm on call all night. It's frost season."

Any jet-setting preconceptions I had about the largest pear grower in the world were obviously wrong. Sue Naumes was a friendly, down-to-earth, dirt-on-her-pants, look-you-straight-in-the-eye farmer—with a law degree.

While we looked over four immense albums of antique fruit labels, Sue talked about farm life. "It's hard work," she said. "I'm out in the orchard all day, every day. It's always a new problem, mechanical or labor. I can't

leave from February to May, even for a night to go to Portland for a show. If there's a frost we have to act quick, respond like firemen, and water the trees to avoid frost damage." Sue, strong, intelligent, and fifty, lives in what was her parents' home overlooking acres of pear trees. She continues to work like her dad, spending long days in work boots doing what needs to be done. Sue learned to move irrigation pipe at age eleven and was picking, thinning, and smudging by eighth grade. Sue proudly remembers her high-school job managing a team of high-school boys with smudge pots.

The Naumes have their own hundred-year heritage, starting with their grandfather, Peter Naumes, who left Chicago and came to Oregon to grow fruit. His son, Joe Naumes, founded the company in 1946, after World War II.

Unlike single-crop growers, the Naumes grow five different fruits, including twenty varieties of pear and Asian pear and ten varieties of apple. Their red pear selection is the most extensive in the industry, and they also offer lesser-known commercial pears like Winter Nélis, Seckels, and Forelles.

Their state-of-the-art orchard has small trees trellised to increase the fruit-bearing surface. Four hundred trees can now grow on an acre that had only seventy trees twenty years ago. Naumes stays on top of the industry with computer-controlled irrigation and fertigation (adding fertilizer to irrigation water). They have their own horticulturists, rootstock nursery, packing

A RED PEAR STORY

Half a century ago, Dr. F. C. Reimer of the Oregon State University Experiment Station planted seeds of a red pear mutant growing on a tree of yellow pears. to find out if the new trees would produce all red pears. The experiment, which took thirty years, resulted in trees that produced bright red Bartlett pears. Young Sue Naumes remembers going hand in hand with her

Dana's Hovey
UNITED STATES, 1854

Believed to be a seedling of Seckel, because of its
close resemblance, this was a seedling pear produced
by Francis Dana of Boston. It ripens in
November, later than Seckel, extending the Seckel
season. Dana's Hovey (often sold as Seckel) is rich,
sharp, and sugary like Seckel, and the
fruit is usually sold as such.

Dearborn
UNITED STATES, 1883 (shown on page 22)

A small, smooth-skinned pear of early American
origin that is nearly extinct. Its flesh is
fine-textured, somewhat dry with no
pronounced aroma.

father, Joe Naumes, to visit Dr. Reimer and his red pears. When he
had proven his hypothesis and was satisfied with his data, he had
no further use for the trees and was ready to discard them. But Joe
Naumes decided to take the rootstock for his commercial orchard.
Today, Joe's company, Naumes, Inc., is the world leader in growing
and developing red pears.

sites, shipping company, and juice-processing plants that convert 600 tons of fruit a day into concentrates.

Though technology has increased yield, pear growing has remained a tough, hands-on business. Like the disappearing small-time farmers, Sue Naumes is caught between consumers wanting 1960's prices despite 2000's costs. "At one time," Sue laments, "the Rogue River Valley had over 400 pear growers, now there are only twenty-six, and a half dozen of those orchards are up for sale." Growers, even big growers, face many difficulties. A sudden frost or a hailstorm can cause quarter-sized holes that can destroy a pear crop. Land laws restrict a farmer's ability to sell off parcels after a bad year. Growers are forced to put those little identification stickers on the fruit so grocery clerks don't have to learn the difference between a Bartlett and an Anjou. Pesticide issues, more regulations, fewer buyers, and a young generation uninterested in working the land are future difficulties for growers. Sue jokes about the many young people she has kept in college because they learned what manual labor was like in her orchard. "Kids today just don't want to do this kind of work," she remarks, looking out over acres of white pear blossoms. "Who will be growing pears in a hundred years?" I ask. "No," corrects Sue, "who will be growing pears in ten?"

Sue Naumes in the orchards of Naumes, Inc., in Medford, Oregon

Devoe

UNITED STATES, 1947

This fruit was first discovered in New York's Hudson
River Valley and is grown only there and in adjacent
states. The fruits ripen early, at the end of summer.
They resemble Bosc in form, with the flesh of a
Bartlett, though lacking Bartlett's characteristic
musky aroma. Devoe is slightly coarse, rather juicy,
and does not keep long in cold storage. Occasionally,
it appears in New York greenmarkets. The flesh does
not withstand cooking, so this pear is suitable for
fresh consumption only.

Duchesse Bronzée
(du-SHES brown-ZAY)

FRANCE, 1808

A sport of the standard Duchesse d'Angoulême,
it produces russeted fruits otherwise identical to its
parent. Russet fruits resist several pear
diseases, and thus are advantageous
for market growers.

*The pear is the symbol for
the human heart.*

—THE DICTIONARY OF MYTHOLOGY,
FOLKLORE, AND SYMBOLS

Duchesse d'Angoulême

(du-SHES dan-gou-LEM) FRANCE, 1870

This French variety dates from the time of Napoleon.
An immense, broad fruit when well grown, it was a
favorite in the eastern United States in the nineteenth
century and is still occasionally grown for its size.
The flesh is somewhat coarse, juicy, acid, and sweet.
Its quality is disappointing when grown in shade or
after rainy summers. It appears in eastern greenmarkets from time to time,
mostly in October.

Easter Beurré

(not pictured) BELGIUM, 1825

A winter pear, Easter Beurré was discovered in a
monastery garden at Louvain. It is large and blocky
with tough, thick skin. The flesh is rather gritty,
acid, and juicy. It must remain on the tree until the
onset of winter, and, if stored under humid conditions,
will develop the melting quality the French
call fondante.

Immature
Bartlett

Flemish Beauty

BELGIUM, 1830

Originally named Fondante de Bois, "candy of the
woods," Flemish Beauty was discovered as a wild
tree in the forest near Aalst, Belgium. Well
named, this variety has a fine, sweet flavor rather
low in acid, a smooth skin, and a consistently
regular shape. It should not be stored long before
eating, as it tends to grow mealy with age. The
Flemish Beauty was one of the six most popular
pears in America in the nineteenth century. Fruits
occasionally show up at stalls in greenmarkets,
often picked from trees planted a
century ago.

Forelle
GERMANY, ANCIENT
(ALSO CALLED
TROUT PEAR)

Forelle is the German word for trout, so named for the red spots on its skin. These spots diffuse gradually into the skin after the fruit is picked, eventually becoming a crimson blush. Its eating quality is only fair. The flesh is smooth, dry, and rather low in acid and sugar. It is an heirloom usually grown because of its great beauty and has only recently been rediscovered by commercial orchardists.

Gorham
NEW YORK, 1910

This is a seedling variety of Bartlett produced when the New York State Experiment Station was active in pear hybridization. Gorham achieved commercial acceptance only in recent decades, and is to be sought as one of the outstanding American fruits. Though not thin-skinned, the Gorham's flesh is smooth, slightly aromatic of conifer woods, juicy, and rich with both sugar and acid. Grand Champion is a russet sport of Gorham, and is even finer for dessert.

Beurré Hardy
(beuh-RAY ar-DEE)

FRANCE, 1820

(ALSO CALLED GELLERT'S BUTTERBIRNE IN
NORTHERN EUROPE, FRENCH BUTTER PEAR)

Hardy is sold in this country as a generic
French Butter pear, but there are actually over
100 varieties that share the name Beurré, or
Butter pear. The name Hardy commemorates the
director of the Luxembourg Gardens at the time of
this pear's introduction. Hardy is uniformly
covered with an attractive russet skin, which
protects the tender, extraordinarily juicy flesh.
It is famous for its pronounced flavor of
rose water.

*T*he exquisite old Butter pears are the family favorites," says Sally Small, who grew up on her grandfather's pear orchard in Walnut Grove, California. In the 1970s, Sally's father wanted to replace the French Butter pears with a more marketable variety, because they were too delicate to be machine packed and could only be sold for baby food.

"Please, give us a season, we'll make this work," Sally and her brother requested. With the family station wagon loaded up with boxes of small golden-green Butter pears, Sally and her brother Rob drove to every restaurant and fruit retailer in the San Francisco area, trying to get buyers to taste their pears. Buyers, unaccustomed to heirloom varieties, thought the fruit was too small and ugly. The fruit was rejected because it didn't shine, like glossy waxed supermarket pears.

But chefs at Chez Panisse and several other Bay Area restaurants felt the superb taste of the Butter pears far outweighed their appearance and encouraged Sally and Rob to continue harvesting. Today, the Pettigrew Fruit Company is a successful orchard growing both the commercially successful Bartletts and the heirloom French and Italian Butter pears. Sally and her brother take pride not only in keeping their grandfather's trees alive, but also the tradition of careful picking and hand wrapping the fruit. "The whole orchard takes on a different tone when we finish with the grueling Bartlett harvest in July. In September everyone slows down for the Butter pear harvest. The men sing more in the orchard. The noise of the packing-house machines stops and women wrap the pears in paper tissue by hand. Everyone smiles more."

Jargonelle

(jar-goh-NEL) ORIGIN UNKNOWN, ANCIENT

This patriarch among pears is believed by some to
be the *Pirum Girgonum* of the Romans, described
at the beginning of the Christian Era and attributed to ancient Greece. It was grown in all pear
countries as the first pear of the season and may be
eaten from the tree as early as July. An ephemeral
fruit, sweet and slightly tart, lasting only a few
days, Jargonelles are occasionally offered for sale,
usually under the mistaken name
of Amiré Joannet.

French Jargonelle

ORIGIN PROBABLY FRANCE, ANCIENT

Introduced to the United States in the nineteenth
century under the misnomer Jargonelle, this fruit
is still sold by nurseries under that name. Though
it resembles the true Jargonelle in its form and
brief season, it ripens well after
Jargonelle and requires cold storage
before ripening. The flesh is very
soft, but unlike Jargonelle,
is not for eating from the tree.
This is a pleasant early
pear, juicy and rather
acid, deserving
an identity of
its own.

*The greatest gift of a garden is the
restoration of the five senses.*

—HANNAH RION

Louise Bonne d'Avranches
(lu-EEZ-uh BOHN dahv-RAHNCH)
(ALSO CALLED LOUISE BONNE OF JERSEY)
NORMANDY, FRANCE, 1780

According to Quintinye, the Versailles
gardener of King Louis XIV, Louise Bonne is
one of the finest French pears. In his writings, he
said that the pear was dedicated to Lady Louise
from the land of Essarts. Louise Bonné often takes
first prize in tasting events, with its perfumed,
very sweet flavor, which is a bit sharp, and its
melting smooth texture. It is a classic autumn
pear, with the characteristic turban shape. Famous
for its fertility, the tree never misses a crop. The
fruit remains in good condition on the
tree for a long period of time.

Madeleine
(not pictured) FRANCE, ANCIENT

The Madeleine popular at the court of Louis
XIII of France is known today in France as

Citron des Carmes, for the Carmelite convent where it was said to have originated. Of notable earliness, Madeleine is rather small, juicy and sweet, and it does not keep well once it is ripe.

Magness
UNITED STATES, 1960

Introduced by the United States Department of Agriculture in Maryland, the Magness is an interesting combination of the delicious Comice and the hardy Seckel, though it resembles Gorham and Anjou more closely. Nicely aromatic, finely textured, and juicy, this pear has been planted in eastern states where other varieties might succumb to diseases. It is worth planting elsewhere because of its high quality. Look for it in greenmarkets, to be used fresh during its autumn season.

Nye Russet

UNITED STATES, 1937

The Nye Russet originated as a sport of Bartlett. It was discovered inthe Oregon orchard of Mr. Stephen Nye in 1937. Its skin is completely covered with russet, and the flesh is as smooth as a Bartlett. Instead of Bartlett's musky aroma, the Nye Russet has a spicy, exotic perfume. It's best used fresh, in the late-summer.

Packham's Triumph

AUSTRALIA, 1897

This progeny of Bartlett much resembles its parent and is often sold as such in the United States. However, Packham is squatter, with coarser flesh and strings around its core, and an even stronger aroma of musk than that of the Bartlett. Often sold abroad as Packham's, this variety ripens over a month after the summer Bartlett and has superior traveling abili-ty. Imported from Chile, the Cape, or New Zealand, it is usually seen in America in late spring.

Passe Crassane

(pass-SEY crah-SAHN)

FRANCE, 1855

This classic winter pear is the finest pear following Comice in January and February. It is found in Paris markets, with stems traditionally dipped in red sealing wax to reduce moisture loss during storage, because it does not store well. The Passe Crassane's skin is rough, thick, and leathery. Its flesh is coarse, rather gritty near the core, very juicy, and decidedly acid, with a citrus flavor. Introduced at Rouen, this variety quickly became famous in France. Nearly all of the crop is now produced in Northern Italy, however.

Petit Muscat
ORIGIN UNKNOWN, ANCIENT
(ALSO CALLED PERRY PEAR)

This uncommon pear is representative of the oldest forms of pears common during the Bronze Age or earlier. The fruits are minute but very juicy, sweet, and pleasant. Petit Muscat has been identified with remains of pears found at sites dating from the Roman Empire, and its Muscat progeny survive today in Northern Europe as local varieties used for fermented perry.

Pound Pear
ENGLAND; BEFORE 1700, PERHAPS ANCIENT
(ALSO CALLED BELLE ANGERINE BELLISSIME d'HIVER, UVEDALE'S ST. GERMAIN)

The Pound Pear, one of the few remaining cooking pears, is grown more for its immense size than its taste. The largest of all pears, it has been known to grow monstrous fruits to over four pounds. Pound is among the last of the pears to be picked before the hard frosts begin. Neither juicy nor remarkably sweet when raw, this pear becomes delicious when cooked. A tradition in England is to bake a whole pear wrapped in a pastry shell. (See recipe page 123.)

Rousselet de Reims

FRANCE, ANCIENT *(pictured on page 5)*

(ALSO CALLED MUSK PEAR, SPICE PEAR)

This small blushed heirloom was the favorite pear of King Luis XIV, and its history has been associated with Reims, France, for centuries. It is sweet, rich, almost melting with the characteristic spicy aroma and caramel flavor of its American offspring, the Seckel. Rousselet is good for candying and desserts. It ripens in late August, two weeks earlier than Seckel.

Seckel

UNITED STATES, 1790

(ALSO CALLED HONEY PEAR OR SUGAR PEAR)

America's gift to the pear world, the Seckel is beloved by pear enthusiasts in the eastern United States because it is so tolerant of diseases and adverse growing conditions, and so productive of usable fruits. Its origins date to the end of the eighteenth century, near Philadelphia and the Seckel appears in the parentage of many modern varieties; The fruit is among the smallest in commerce, and does not travel or keep long, especially at supermarket temperatures. It is fine textured, juicy, and syrupy, making it ideal for sorbets, eating fresh, and poaching. It also makes delicious preserves and baked goods.

Beurré Superfin

(beuh-RAY super-FAHN) FRANCE, 1840

Superfin is among the very finest of all pears,
yet it is little known in this country. It has an
exquisite, sweet-tart flavor. Its aroma is not
pronounced, but is more noticeable when cut open.
Planted occasionally in the United States, chiefly
as a pollinator in orchards of
Bartletts, Superfin fruits
have been used chiefly for juice,
as a base for stronger flavored
fruits and tea in bottled
beverages.

Warden

(not pictured) ENGLAND, ANCIENT

The Warden is not strictly a variety of pear, but
rather the name of a class of cooking pears that
has nearly vanished. True Wardens are dense,
hard-fleshed pears, usually dark green and bitter,
but if cooked, they turn a marvelously deep pink,
soft and sweet, with a spicy aroma. Probably the
only true Warden surviving today is the Black
Worcester, dating back to the twelfth century at
latest, that appears on the arms of
that English city.

White Doyenné

(DOY-eh-nay) ITALY, BEFORE 1550

Outstandingly juicy when well grown,
this sweet and rich dessert pear is a favorite of fruit
collectors. A characteristic egg-shaped fruit, always a
clear yellow when fully ripe, it remains well appreciated for its dependably generous fruit production.
This pear may be eaten off the tree when mature,
but improves with cold storage.

Winter Nélis

BELGIUM, 1804 (ALSO CALLED
BONNE DE MALINES)

This pear commemorates Jean-
Charles Nélis of Mechelen,
Belgium, a pear fancier of
the early nineteenth century.
This is the only true winter
pear to survive in American
commerce. The skin is thick
and coarse, and the flesh is
slightly greenish, fine, extra
ordinarily rich, and not
gritty. The syrupy juice has
a distinct sharpness. Winter
Nélises must remain on the tree
until leaf-fall, usually November.

ASIAN PEARS

PYRUS PYRIFOLIA OR P. USSURIENSIS VAR. OVOIDEA

Asian pears are often called apple pears, because of their apple shape and crunchy texture, or sand pears for their numerous grit cells, but they are not a cross between an apple and a pear. They are members of various true pear species called Li in China and Nashi in Japan. In Asia, pears are never cooked, but always eaten fresh. However, America's favorite cooking pear, the Kieffer, is actually a European and Asian hybrid.

Chojuro
JAPAN, 1895

The Chojuro is always eaten peeled, as its russet skin is very thick. The flesh is rather coarse, dense, and dry by modern standards, remarkably aromatic before storage, but not particularly sweet. Chojuro is available from late August through December and is valued for its long-keeping qualities.

Hosui

JAPAN, 1954

The late-fall Hosui is currently considered to be
the standard of high quality in Japanese pears. The
skin is thinner than that of older types of Nashi,
but it still must be peeled. Hosui (the word means
"copious juice") is outstandingly juicy, with sweet
flesh, and is only moderately aromatic.

He who plants a garden,
plants happiness.

—CHINESE PROVERB

Kieffer
UNITED STATES, 1863

Actually a hybrid of a Japanese Nashi and a
European pear, the Kieffer is of a class called sand
pears, common in the American South, where other
pears will not thrive. The Kieffer is often used for
canning. Typically, the hard flesh is bitter and does
not soften after harvest, but if grown in a long season and allowed to remain on the
tree, the flesh becomes pleasant to eat
as a dessert.

THE PEAR BIBLE

In 1921, U. P. Hedrick wrote the classic text The
Pears of New York to give an account of "the botanical
characters of cultivated pears . . . in the United States." Part
of a botanical series on fruit published by the New York
Agricultural Experiment Station, the book contains color plates of
eighty cultivated pears and descriptions of over eight hundred more,
most of which were extinct by 1900. Today the text is regarded
by botanists and rare book collectors as the pear bible. Though out of
print, the exquisite color plates, actually colorized photos, not drawings,
can be viewed on the Internet at www.ars-grin.gov/cor/pony.html.

Okusankishi

(ALSO CALLED NIHON NASHI, BANSAN KICHI)

JAPAN, 1890'S

Though this Nashi is obsolete in Japan, it is one of the oldest varieties still cultivated in California. For optimum juiciness it should be stored for only a few weeks. Its flesh is rather course, but its subtle flavor is both sweet and tart.

KIEFFER

Shinko

JAPAN, 1934

The Shinko comes from a Japanese breeding program. Its name means "novelty." Appreciated for
handsome russeted skin, Shinko has dense, firm
flesh that is somewhat juicy when at its best. This
Nashi, available in early October, is better peeled,
because its skin is somewhat bitter. It is not suitable for long storage.

Asian Pear Leaf

Shinseiki
JAPAN, 1945

This Japanese hybrid is one of the
most popular Nashi; its skin is usually peeled.
It is very juicy, rather sweet, and relieved by acidity (especially near the core). Shinseiki (which
means "new century") is the earliest of the
Nashi, generally available in late summer.
It tastes best when tree-ripened.

European Pear Leaf

Tarusa Crimson
(ALSO CALLED TAMARED)
NEW ZEALAND, 1972

A New Zealand sand pear hybrid, this pear is
grown for its remarkable clear red color, unique
among Asian pears. Its flesh is rather dry and
somewhat aromatic, but it is less sweet
than most Nashi.

*If you can spend
a perfectly useless afternoon
in a perfectly useless manner,
you have learned how to live.*

—LIN YÜ-T'ANG (1895–1976),
CHINESE WRITER AND PHILOLOGIST

Tsu Li

CHINA, ANCIENT

This is typical of the Chinese form of the
Asian pear, called Li. A timeless variety from
China, the Tsu Li is probably 1,000 years
old or older. Its skin is speckled with
russet, which distinguishes it from Ya Li.
The flesh is decidedly dry, making
this a long-keeping fruit. It is
a traditional fruit for
lunar new year
celebrations.

A Chinese "Pearable"

ruthless Chinese militarist, Tsíao Tsíao, decided to build a great palace for himself. In order to obtain a large pillar, he ordered a pear tree to be cut down. Whenever his worker's ax struck the tree, however, the tree let out a groan. The frightened worker ceased chopping and reported the occurrence. Tsíao Tsíao was so angry he decided to cut the tree down himself, but was splashed with blood at his first stroke. During the following night, the spirit of the tree visited him and, after reprimanding Tsíao Tsíao for his brutality, struck him a blow on the head. The blow threw Tsíao Tsíao into a delirium, during which the spirits of people he had slain tormented him. He never recovered.

Twentieth Century
(NIJISEIKI) JAPAN, 1898

Everyone's favorite Nashi, or Japanese pear. It is exceptionally juicy and sweet, but not aromatic. It has some sharpness when not harvested too late. The skin has a characteristic greasy feel. It is the second-earliest Asian pear, after Shinseiki.

Ya Li

CHINA, ANCIENT

The name Ya Li means "duck bill," after the curve of this pear's neckline. The Ya Li has dryer flesh than most Nashi. It is more aromatic and higher in sugars, holding acidity longer. A form of ancient Li (Chinese pear), it is available at the new year in every Chinese community.

PEAR TASTING GLOSSARY

TERM	VARIETAL EXAMPLES
AROMATIC	*Beurré Hardy (rose water aroma), Rousselet de Reims Bartlett, (musk), Seckel (sp*.
ASTRINGENT	
BUTTERY	*Comice, White Doyenné, Conference*
COMPLEX	*Seckel, Winter Nélis*
CRISP	*Kieffer, Twentieth Century, Shinseiki*
COOKING PEAR	*Kieffer, Pound pear (Belle Angevine)*
DESSERT PEAR	*Comice, Anjou, Beurré Hardy*
EAU-DE-VIE	
FINE GRAINED	*Flemish Beauty*
FLESH	
FONDANTE	*Fondante d'Automne (Belle Lucrative)*
GRIT CELLS	*Winter Nélis, Passe Crassane, Hosui, Ya Li*
JUICE	*Conference, Seckel, Twentieth Century*
MELTING	*Anjou, Comice, White Doyenné*
MUSK	*Bartlett, Packham's Triumph*
NUTLIKE	*Bosc, Winter Nélis, Louise Bonne*
PERFUME	
RICH	*Comice, White Doyenné, Louise Bonne*
SPICE	*Seckel, Bosc, Rousselet de Reims*
SUBACID	*Louise Bonne, Passe Crassane*
SWEETNESS	*Seckel, Rousselet de Reims, Clapp's Favorite*
TART	*Bartlett*
TEXTURE	
VINOUS	*Glou Morceau, Passe Crassanne*
WINE-LIKE	*White Doyenné, Comice, French Butter pears*

DEFINITION

The presence of a distinct perfume in fully ripe Bartlett pears; may be of citrus, musk, spice, or other scents

The bitter flavor of tannins, which are present in the skin of pears and all immature fruit. (*See also* nutlike.)

Also beurré, French adjective for "buttery," which comes from the combination of smooth flesh and high juice content found in the finest varieties.

A combination of many distinguishable aromas and flavors; a desirable characteristic of fine fruit.

Flesh breaking to the bite; a quality favored only in Asian pears and Asian/European hybrids.

Bland, often hard, fruits that improve in flavor and texture only when cooked. Used for canning and preserves.

A sweet, fine-textured, rich-flavored pear for eating out of hand.

French for "water of life;" a clear liqueur made from fruit juice, similar to cognac. Pear eau-de-vie is commercially called Poire William.

The texture of the flesh, not the juice. Absence of grit cells.

The meat of the pear; white to yellow-white in color. Immature pears have greenish flesh.

Culinary French meaning "to melt in the mouth"; see also *melting*.

A granular silica found in pears; associated with firm, dense texture. Flesh without grit liquefies or melts in the mouth when ripe.

A byproduct of cell breakdown in the ripening process. Dessert pears are evaluated by their juiciness, texture and richness.

Smooth, fine texture, in combination with high juice content; found in dessert pears; tender.

A characteristic aroma of certain dessert pears.

A distinct astringency contributing to complex flavor.

See *aromatic*.

Said only of pears high in both sugar and acid.

A complex aroma suggestive of nutmeg, cinnamon, and clove.

Decidedly sharp or biting.

Sugar content; lacking in bitterness. A Seckel can average 15 percent sugar content and a Hosui Asian pear 12 percent.

Higher in acid than in sugar; more noticeably tart than sweet.

A condition of the flesh when eaten; ranges from smooth and melting in dessert pears to dense and crisp in Asian pears.

Literally "taste of the vine," an herbaceous green taste of chlorophyll, usually associated with astringency. Common in immature fruits, this taste is often mistaken for winelike.

A layperson's term likening the rich flavor of fine dessert pears to wine.

Pears
in the
Kitchen

*Tall-stemmed Bosc poaching in
red wine and spices.*

IN THE KITCHEN

That's not cooking, that's shopping.

—A CHEF'S COMMENT
TO ALICE WATERS

To experience ripe pears at their finest, consumers need patience, a delicate touch, and the knowledge of what to look for in the market.

How to Tell if a Pear Is Ripe

Sniff the pear for a strong perfume and gently press the stem end with your thumb. If it yields to pressure, this tells you that the pear is already ripe and flavorful. A ripe pear has undergone a sugar conversion process and, at its peak, is sweet and juicy with a fine texture. Ripe pears should be eaten right away, but they will keep in the refrigerator for a few days. Left out at room temperature, ripe pears will quickly turn soft and mushy.

Home-Ripening Pears

Planning ahead is an important part of using pears. Commercial pears are picked when mature (when the seeds are brown and ready to germinate), but they need additional storage time to mature in taste, texture, and juiciness. Most varieties go into a 34-degree cold storage and arrive at the market rock hard, but they can be ripened in your kitchen. During the ripening process, the bitterness breaks down and the aromatics are released. Choose pears that are firm, without cuts or bruises, with the stem intact. Even unripe pears should be handled gently. Though an unripe pear will not show a bruise, a brown mark will appear on the skin as it begins to ripen. Pears taken home are best ripened standing up in an uncrowded bowl or in a paper bag. It may take a couple days or up to a week. If a pear refuses to ripen but stays hard with an off color, it was probably picked too soon.

To hurry the ripening process, put pears in a plastic bag with a banana or a cut apple and the ethylene gas produced will speed the ripening. Remember fresh fruit continues to breathe, taking up CO_2 and releasing oxygen as it ripens and eventually decays. You can prolong the peak condition of pears by chilling them. The next best thing to a ventilated fruit cellar is an old refrigerator that does not use a vacuum, which draws out flavor and moisture.

The Season for Pears

Look for pears in season from local markets starting in mid-July and through autumn for Anjou, Bosc, and Comice. The season ends in January, with Winter Nélis, the only true winter pear in the United States. After February, the pears in the United States market come from South America (usually Chile or Argentina) or have been kept in controlled atmosphere (CA) storage. In CA storage, the carbon dioxide levels have been substantially reduced and nitrogen levels increased to lengthen the pears' cold storage time, so that West Coast pears will be available in the stores until May. The fruit is unharmed but held in a suspended state until taken out.

Pear Nutrition

Pears contain more levulose, the sweetest of known sugars, than any other fruit. They are also high in potassium and low in calories. A medium-sized pear has 98 calories and 208 milligrams of potassium, and pear skins provide valuable fiber.

Finding Gourmet Pears

For the truly elite varieties, like the White Doyenné or the Belle Lucrative, one must grow the trees. However, very good pears can be found in shops specializing in fine fruits or by strolling the local markets looking for organically grown pears and asking for a taste. You may discover a grower's old family heirloom that is making a comeback.

Among the standard varieties, experts claim the best-tasting commercial pear is Comice, the same golden-blushed pear that's wrapped in tissue in mail-order fruit baskets. When perfectly ripe, the Comice is buttery and sweet, with a winelike tartness and flesh that melts in your mouth. Look for it starting in November. A ripe Comice is large and often scratched with pale brown or dull green markings.

To fully appreciate the taste of fresh pears, always peel them. Try slices on crusty French bread with Gorgonzola or creamy mascarpone. To help peeled pears hold their color, refrigerate them before peeling and squeeze lemon juice on the peeled slices. Then toss them in salads with pecans or walnuts and a strong cheese like Parmesan, blue, or feta. Smooth-textured pears like Comice make excellent sorbets. Asian pears are crisp when ripe and are best eaten fresh.

Peeling and Coring

Most cooking recipes call for peeled, cored pears. Peeling a nearly ripe pear is easier than peeling a potato or an apple. The blade of a vegetable peeler knows exactly where to go so the skin falls away evenly in one piece without much effort or waste of pear. The easiest way to core a pear is to use a melon baller. Insert the small end into the bottom end of the pear and, with several twists, neatly remove the seeds. To stuff pears, slice them vertically, remove the stem and the fibrous cord running through the pear core, and use a melon baller to remove the seeds, making a neat round hole to stuff with cottage cheese, Gorgonzola, or a favorite dessert topping.

Cooking with Pears

The all-around favorite cooking pear has to be the Bosc. Its tall, sensuous body and rich, nutty fall flavor are perfect for showy desserts like standing wine-poached pears or a spiral of burgundy slices in a pastry shell.

All commercial pears bake well, and their flavor is enhanced when they are cooked in pastries and breads or simply added to hot oatmeal. Even unripe pears become delicious when baked or poached with wine. Try adding pears to your favorite broiled meat dishes. Sweet pear juices flavor salad dressings, sauces, gelatins, and chutneys. When cooking with pears, remember that slightly underripe, firm fruit holds up better when peeled, baked, and poached. Poaching pears (page 130) in red wine or grape juice will turn them a deep bur-

gundy for a special dessert. For red color throughout, marinate thick pear slices or small whole
Seckel pears in red wine or grape juice overnight.

Dried Pears

For thousands of years, pears have been
preseved by drying and canning, but not
freezing, which causes the juice to separate upon thawing. Dried pears store the
sun's energy in concentrated form. Preserved
fruit helped our ancestors survive through bleak win-
ters and times of famine, and dried fruit was a traditional fast food for long journeys. Dried pears are
high in sugar and rich in nutrients, especially potassium and vitamin C. An old tradition, especially in
warm climates, is to dry fruit on large trays on
rooftops (see recipe, page 140). On a hot day, the
fruit can dry in hours. But expect to share the harvest with a few of nature's creatures who drop by for
a sample.

How did the pear get in the bottle? The bottles are actually placed over the tiny fruits on the tree after the blossoms drop in the spring. The bottles are sealed, and the fruit is allowed to grow to maturity inside. The bottle and fruit are then removed from the tree in the fall and filled with pear eau-de-vie.

PERRY AND LIQUEURS

Perry

Perry is to pears what cider is to apples. Although the chemistry of fermentation in making perry is beyond the scope of this book, future perry makers may like to know that it takes 20 pounds of whole, unpeeled pears to yield a gallon of juice. Traditionally, British perry is made with small, bitter, unpalatable pears.

Pear Eau-de-vie (Poire William)

Pear eau-de-vie is a crystal-clear cognaclike liqueur often sold with a whole pear inside a tall narrow-necked bottle. It is made from the strong-fragranced pear the French call Williams Bon-Chretien or, more commonly, Bartlett. It takes twenty-eight pounds of pears to yield a single bottle of eau-de-vie. Small farmers who create specialty procducts, like pear-in-the-bottle eau-de-vie and exclusive olive oils, have found innovative ways to keep old orchards alive and producing.

Make your own Red Bartlett Liqueur

Place a red-skinned pear that has been pierced all over with a sharp fork in a wide-mouth quart jar with a tight lid. Fill the jar with vodka, leaving some headroom; cover the jar tightly and store at room temperature for 1 month. Add sugar, mix gently, replace the lid, and store for 3 to 6 months. Add $1/4$ to $1/2$ cup pear eau-de-vie, mix gently, and serve.

Recipes

Mark Miller's Pear and
Black Olive Salsa, page 143

BALSAMIC PEAR-SALMON SAUTÉ

SERVES 2

This one-pan dish can be ready in 30 minutes. Accompany with a wild and brown rice pilaf.

- **2** SALMON STEAKS, ABOUT **4** OUNCES EACH
- **1/4** TEASPOON SALT
- **1/2** TEASPOON FRESHLY GROUND BLACK PEPPER
- **1** TEASPOON UNSALTED BUTTER
- **4** SHALLOTS, THINLY SLICED
- **1** GARLIC CLOVE, THINLY SLICED
- **2** LARGE RIPE BARTLETT OR BOSC PEARS, CORED, PEELED, AND HALVED
- **1/4** TEASPOON FENNEL SEED
- **1/4** CUP PEAR EAU-DE-VIE
- **1/4** CUP BALSAMIC VINEGAR
- FRESH FLAT-LEAF PARSLEY SPRIGS FOR GARNISH

Pat the steaks dry with a paper towel, then season with the salt and pepper. Set aside. Preheat a large nonstick skillet over medium-high heat. Coat the skillet with the butter and heat until the butter foams. Add the steaks. Arrange the shallots, garlic, and the pear halves, cut side down, around the steaks. Cook for about 5 minutes, or until the steaks are brown on one side, then turn. Sprinkle the fennel seed over all.

Mix the eau-de-vie and vinegar in a cup, then pour it over the steaks. Cook for about 3 to 5 minutes longer, or until the steaks are done, the pears are tender, and the liquid has reduced to a thick dark syrup.

Serve each salmon steak with 2 pear halves and a topping of the balsamic syrup. Garnish with a generous amount of parsley.

From Pears *by Linda West Eckhardt (San Francisco, CA: Chronicle Books, 1996).*

GRILLED BARTLETTS AND GINGERED PORK CHOPS

SERVES 4

Pears are delicious grilled, especially when the sweet pear juices blend with the flavors of pork, garlic, ginger, and orange.

- **2** LARGE GARLIC CLOVES, CRUSHED
- **2** TABLESPOONS FINELY GRATED FRESH GINGER
- **1** TABLESPOON GRATED LEMON ZEST
- **SALT AND FRESHLY GROUND BLACK PEPPER** TO TASTE
- **4** RIB PORK CHOPS, **3/4-INCH-THICK,** TRIMMED OF FAT
- **4** FIRM, RIPE PEARS PEELED, HALVED, AND CORED
- **2** TABLESPOONS BUTTER MELTED
- **1/4** CUP ORANGE MARMALADE

Preheat the broiler. In a small bowl, make a marinade of the garlic, ginger, lemon zest, salt, and pepper. Coat both sides of the pork chops with the mixture and set them aside for 15 minutes. Prepare the pear halves and toss them in a bowl with the melted butter to coat. Place the pear halves (cut side down) and chops on a broiler rack. Broil for 5 minutes. Turn both pears and chops. Place $1/2$ teaspoon orange marmalade in each pear and brush the remaining marmalade over the pork chops. Broil another 2 to 3 minutes, or until the pork is cooked through and the pears are lightly browned. Serve the pork chops topped with the grilled pears and cooking juices.

BOSC PIZZETTAS WITH CARAMELIZED SHALLOTS, ARUGULA, AND GRUYÈRE CHEESE

SERVES 4 AS AN ENTRÉE OR 8 AS AN APPETIZER

Boscs are wonderful with cheese, so why not make pizzettas with them? This recipe from Samantha Beers calls for a tangy Gruyère, but a semihard goat cheese would also work. For a summer variation, try pairing Bartletts with an aged Cheddar.

- 2 TABLESPOONS BUTTER
- 3 LARGE SHALLOTS, THINLY SLICED
- 1 TEASPOON HONEY
- PINCH OF SALT AND FRESHLY GROUND BLACK PEPPER
- 1/4 CUP CORNMEAL FOR BAKING
- PIZZETTA DOUGH (RECIPE FOLLOWS)
- 1 SMALL BUNCH OF ARUGULA, WASHED AND TORN INTO LARGE BITS
- 1 FIRM, RIPE BOSC PEAR, PEELED, CORED, AND THINLY SLICED
- 3 OUNCES GRUYÈRE CHEESE, THINLY SLICED (NOT GRATED)

Preheat the oven to 450°. In a small skillet, melt the butter. Add the shallots and cook briefly over high heat. Lower the heat and continue cooking until the shallots turn a rich golden brown. Add the honey, a generous pinch of salt, and a dash of pepper. Cook for 1 more minute, or until a glaze forms, then remove from heat. Sprinkle an oiled baking sheet with cornmeal and arrange 4 rounds of pizzetta dough on top. Spread one fourth of the shallot mixture evenly over each round, followed by the arugula, 3 or 4 pear slices, and the cheese. Bake the pizzettas on the bottom rack of the oven for 8 to 12 minutes, or until the crust is golden and the cheese bubbling. Remove the pizzettas from the oven and serve them as a light late-summer lunch with salad and a dry Gewürztraminer.

PIZZETTA DOUGH

MAKES FOUR 6- TO 7-INCH ROUNDS

2¹/₂ TEASPOONS ACTIVE DRY YEAST

1 TEASPOON SUGAR

2 TABLESPOONS WALNUT OIL

¹/₄ CUP FINELY CHOPPED TOASTED WALNUTS
(OPTIONAL)

2 CUPS UNBLEACHED FLOUR
(PLUS EXTRA FOR KNEADING)

¹/₂ TEASPOON SALT

In a large bowl, proof the yeast with the sugar in ¹/₃ cup lukewarm water for 10 minutes, or until it is foamy. Stir in an additional ¹/₃ cup lukewarm water and the walnut oil, walnuts, flour, and salt. Blend to form a dough. Turn the dough onto a floured surface and knead, gradually adding up to ¹/₄ cup more flour as necessary to prevent sticking. Knead for 5 to 10 minutes, or until the dough is smooth and elastic; it will begin to feel like it is pushing back. Place the dough in an oiled bowl and turn it to coat it with the oil. Let it rise, covered with plastic wrap, in a warm place for 1 hour, or until it is double in size. Now punch it down and divide it into 4 equal portions. On a lightly floured board, form four 6- to 7-inch rounds for pizzettas.

Die Winter-Christbirn
Bon-Chretien d'hiver.

BALSAMIC-MARINATED CHICKEN BREASTS WITH PEARS

SERVES 4

Also from Samantha Beers is a rich late-fall dish to serve with mixed jasmine and brown rice. With some simple greens and a good pinot noir, you have a gorgeous meal for four.

4 BONELESS, SKINLESS CHICKEN BREASTS

MARINADE

1/4 CUP BALSAMIC VINEGAR

1/3 CUP FULL-BODIED DRY RED WINE

1/4 ONION, CUT INTO THIN ROUNDS

2 TABLESPOONS CANOLA OIL

1 TEASPOON DRY BASIL

1/2 TEASPOON CRUMBLED ROSEMARY

1 TABLESPOON SUGAR

1 TEASPOON SALT

1/2 TEASPOON FRESHLY GROUND BLACK PEPPER

2 TABLESPOONS BUTTER

1 CUP CHICKEN STOCK

**2 FIRM, RIPE BOSC OR BARTLETT PEARS,
PEELED, CORED, AND THINLY SLICED**

1/4 CUP HALF-AND-HALF

Wash the chicken and pat it dry. To make the marinade, combine all the marinade ingredients in a bowl with the chicken, mixing well. Cover with plastic wrap and refrigerate for at least 4 hours, stirring once or twice.

Melt the butter in a skillet and add the chicken and the onions from the marinade. Cook the chicken over high heat for 2 or 3 minutes on each side, searing the meat. Add the marinade, reduce heat to medium, cover, and cook for 7 to 10 minutes, adding chicken stock as necessary to prevent drying. When a knife inserted into the center of the meat reveals no remaining pink, transfer the chicken to a heated plate and cover it to keep it moist.

Add the pears and remaining stock to the onions and pan juices, stirring constantly. Raise the heat to reduce the sauce and poach the pears simultaneously. When the sauce has begun to thicken and the pears are translucent and have taken on the color of the sauce, turn the heat to low and add the half-and-half. Return the chicken to the skillet. Cover and let everything simmer for 1 more minute.

SPARERIBS PILLY-MINTON

SERVES 4

This is a nostalgic 1957 Sunset *recipe named for Chef Robert Bard's cat. Bard was called away to the telephone while he was cooking this dish. When he came back, he found that his Siamese cat, named Pilly-Minton, had eaten all but the bones. Though the recipe calls for the canned pears popular in the fifties, it comes with high recommendations from Chez Panisse pastry chef Lindsey Shere.*

1 SIDE OF SPARERIBS

1 TEASPOON DRIED OREGANO

1 TEASPOON DRIED THYME

1 TEASPOON SALT

1/3 CUP ALL PURPOSE FLOUR

1 TABLESPOON DRY GINGER

1/3 CUP PACKED BROWN SUGAR

JUICE FROM 1 (12-OUNCE) CAN BARTLETT PEARS

Preheat the oven to 350°. Put the spareribs rounded side up in a roasting pan and dust them with the oregano, thyme, and salt. Bake the ribs for 1 hour. Remove the pan from the oven and pour off all the fat. Dredge the ribs in the flour, the ginger, then the brown sugar. Put the ribs back in the pan and pour over the pear juice. Bake until the ribs are very brown, about 1 1/2 hours more, turning and basting several times.

From Cooking Bold and Fearless: Chefs of the West *(Menlo Park, CA: Sunset Publishing Corporation, 1957).*

WINTER SECKEL SALAD

SERVES 10

This green-and-red salad with pears and pecans is perfect for late-fall and winter holidays. Make the dressing first so that the pear juices will flavor the dressing.

1/2 CUP PECANS, COARSELY CHOPPED

PEAR DRESSING

2 TABLESPOONS WHITE WINE VINEGAR

1 TABLESPOON BALSAMIC VINEGAR

2 TEASPOONS DIJON MUSTARD

1/2 TEASPOON SALT

1/4 TEASPOON FRESHLY GROUND BLACK PEPPER

1/3 CUP EXTRA VIRGIN OLIVE OIL

4 RIPE SECKEL OR BOSC PEARS,
    PEELED, CORED, AND CUT INTO THIN WEDGES

1 HEAD BUTTER LETTUCE

1 SMALL HEAD RADICCHIO

2 BUNCHES ARUGULA (4 OUNCES EACH)

1/2 CUP COARSELY GRATED PARMESAN CHEESE

Preheat the oven to 350°. Toast the pecan pieces in the oven for 7 to 8 minutes.

To make the dressing, mix the vinegars, mustard, salt, and pepper together in a large bowl. Gradually whisk in the olive oil until blended. Add the pear wedges and coat the pears with dressing. Set aside for at least 15 minutes.

Tear the lettuce, radicchio, and arugula leaves into bite-sized pieces. Put the torn salad greens in a large bowl. Add the toasted pecans and grated Parmesan. Just before serving, toss the greens gently with the dressing.

NOTE: REVIVE TIRED AND SAGGY GREENS IN A BOWL OF CHILLED WATER FOR 30 MINUTES BEFORE MAKING YOUR SALAD.

GORGONZOLA-BARTLETT SALAD

SERVES 6

This twist on a classic Gorgonzola and pear salad uses sundried tomatoes and currants.

1/2 CUP WALNUTS OR PECANS

DRESSING

1/2 CUP EXTRA VIRGIN OLIVE OIL

1 TEASPOON SALT

1 CLOVE GARLIC, PRESSED OR MINCED

2 TABLESPOONS WHITE WINE VINEGAR

2 TABLESPOONS FRESH LEMON JUICE

FRESHLY GROUND BLACK PEPPER TO TASTE

**1 LARGE BUNCH RED LEAF LETTUCE,
    TORN INTO PIECES**

**1/2 CUP DRY-PACKED SUN-DRIED TOMATOES,
    QUARTERED AND SOAKED IN WATER
    FOR 30 MINUTES**

1/2 SMALL RED ONION, SLICED PAPER THIN

1/2 CUP DRIED CURRANTS

1/4 CUP CHOPPED FRESH PARSLEY

**3 FIRM, RIPE CHILLED BARTLETTS, PEELED,
    CORED AND CUT INTO 1/2 -INCH PIECES**

3 OUNCES GORGONZOLA CHEESE, CRUMBLED

Preheat the oven to 325°. Toast the walnuts in the oven for 7 to 8 minutes.

Mix the dressing ingredients in a container with a tightly fitting lid. Fasten the lid and shake vigorously.

Toss the lettuce in a large salad bowl with the sundried tomatoes, onion, currants, and parsley. Add the pears to the salad and mix with the dressing. Arrange the salad on a dinner plate. Top with the warm walnuts and chunks of Gorgonzola cheese. Serve with a crusty French bread.

CELERIAC AND ASIAN PEAR SALAD

SERVES 6

Celeriac, or celery root, is soft and almost creamy when served with this tart honey-mustard dressing.

2 TABLESPOONS TOASTED SUNFLOWER SEEDS

DRESSING
3 TABLESPOONS MAYONNAISE

3 TABLESPOONS SOUR CREAM

3 TABLESPOONS FRESH LEMON JUICE

1 TABLESPOON DIJON MUSTARD

1 TABLESPOON HONEY

1 TEASPOON SALT

FRESHLY GROUND BLACK PEPPER TO TASTE

1 POUND CELERIAC, PEELED AND SHREDDED IN A FOOD PROCESSOR TO LOOK LIKE SPAGHETTI

1 HOSUI OR SHINSEIKI ASIAN PEAR, PEELED, CORED, AND SHREDDED IN A FOOD PROCESSOR

CHOPPED FRESH CHIVES FOR GARNISH

Preheat the oven to 325°. Toast the sunflower seeds in the oven for 7 to 8 minutes.

To make the dressing, combine the dressing ingredients in a small bowl.

Add the dressing to the celeriac immediately after shredding, to avoid discoloration. Stir in the Asian pear and sunflower seeds and garnish with chives. The salad is best if refrigerated for several hours.

SPICED BOSC PEAR AND PEPPER JACK SOUP

SERVES 8

La Casa Sena, the well-known Santa Fe restaurant, developed this Southwest-style soup with winter Bosc pears. Centuries ago the Spanish planted orchards of Bosc in the Rio Grande Valley, and many are still producing fruit today.

7 BOSC PEARS, PEELED, SEEDED, AND DICED

2 QUARTS CHICKEN STOCK

1/2 TABLESPOON HONEY

PINCH OF PURE GROUND CHILE

PINCH OF GROUND NUTMEG

PINCH OF GROUND CINNAMON

SALT AND FRESHLY GROUND WHITE PEPPER TO TASTE

1 CUP HEAVY CREAM

1/2 CUP SHREDDED PEPPER JACK CHEESE FOR GARNISH

1/2 CUP CRUMBLED CRISP BACON FOR GARNISH

In a saucepan, combine the pears, stock, honey, ground chile, nutmeg, cinnamon, salt, and pepper. Bring the mixture to a boil, decrease the heat, and simmer for 4 or 5 minutes, or until the pears are soft. Transfer the mixture to a food processor or blender and purée until smooth. Blend in the cream.

Serve the soup in bowls, sprinkled with the grated cheese and bacon.

From La Casa Sena: The Cuisine of Santa Fe *by Gordon Heiss and John Harrisson (Berkeley, CA: Ten Speed Press, 1994).*

SPICED CARAMEL-BAKED SECKELS

SERVES 4

*As an accompaniment to an entrée of pork or poultry, try these
sweet, appealing little seckels.*

1/4 CUP PACKED BROWN SUGAR

4 TABLESPOONS BUTTER

1/4 CUP DRY WHITE WINE OR WHITE GRAPE JUICE

1/2 SPLIT VANILLA BEAN, SCRAPED

1/2 TEASPOON GROUND CINNAMON

1/4 TEASPOON GROUND GINGER

4 *EACH* WHOLE CLOVES AND PEPPERCORNS

**8 FIRM, RIPE SECKELS, OR 4 LARGER PEARS,
PEELED AND CORED, WITH STEMS INTACT**

Preheat the oven to 350°. To make caramel: Put the
butter, sugar, wine, and spices in a baking pan and
heat in the oven for 5 minutes or until the butter is
melted. Remove from the oven and stir. Place the
pears upright in a baking dish (taking a slice from
their bottom side will help them sit straight). Pour
the caramel over each pear. Bake for 20 minutes,
basting several times. The pears are done when a
knife pierces them easily.

Before serving, pour the juice into a saucepan and
cook for several minutes until thickened. Pour the
juice over the pears and serve.

*There was a time when people ate
350 different plants in a year, now
the number is less than 50.*

—MARKHAM REGIONAL ARBORETUM SOCIETY

PEARS STUFFED WITH GORGONZOLA AND WRAPPED WITH PROSCIUTTO

SERVES 4

A thank you to pear grower Suzanne Adams from Healdsburg, California, the heart of pear country, for this simple but delicious appetizer.

2 LARGE PEARS, PEELED
4 OUNCES GORGONZOLA CHEESE
16 PIECES THINLY SLICED PROSCIUTTO

Preheat the oven to 400°. Cut the pears in half. Remove the stringy part of the core by pulling down on the stem toward the center. Using a melon baller, remove the core. Fill the cups of each half with Gorgonzola. Carefully slice the halved pears lengthwise into 4 spears, so that you end up with 16 pieces. Wrap each pear snugly in a slice of prosciutto. Bake for 10 minutes. Serve with toothpicks.

OPEN-FACE COMICE AND GORGONZOLA SANDWICHES

SERVES 6

A perfect marriage: ripe Comice and rich Gorgonzola.

4 OUNCES GORGONZOLA CHEESE
3 OUNCES CREAM CHEESE, SOFTENED
1/2 LOAF CRUSTY SOURDOUGH FRENCH BREAD, CUT INTO 6 1/2-INCH SLICES
2 RIPE COMICE PEARS, PEELED, CORED, AND SLICED
1 BUNCH ARUGULA

Blend the Gorgonzola into the cream cheese. A tablespoon of milk can be added if a softer spread is desired. If the Gorgonzola is too strong for your taste, try thinning it with more cream cheese. Spread the bread with the cheese mixture. Layer on slices of pear and garnish with arugula leaves. Yum!

GRILLED PEAR, CHILE, AND ASIAGO QUESADILLAS

MAKES 4 QUESADILLAS

Pears not only go great in salsas, but here, they are pan-roasted along with chiles and placed in a quesadilla.

3 NEW MEXICO GREEN CHILES

2 FIRM, RIPE BOSC PEARS, PEELED AND CORED

4 (10-INCH) FLOUR TORTILLAS

1 1/2 CUPS GRATED ASIAGO CHEESE

1/4 CUP CHOPPED FRESH CILANTRO

1 TABLESPOON BUTTER

1 TOMATO, CHOPPED

JUICE OF 1/2 LIME

CHOPPED FRESH CILANTRO TO TASTE

SALT TO TASTE

Place the chiles and pears in an oiled skillet over low heat. Cook, turning occasionally, until the chiles are charred and the pears are browned, 20 to 30 minutes. Wrap the chiles in damp paper towels and place them in a plastic bag for 10 minutes. Then remove the peel, stem end, and inner seed pod. Cut the chiles into long strips and the pears into small 1/2-inch pieces.

On a clean skillet over medium-high heat, cook a flour tortilla until the skin begins to bubble. Turn the tortilla and add a few strips of chili, one fourth of the pear pieces and the Asiago cheese, and a sprinkle of cilantro. (If the chiles are very hot, use sparingly.) Fold the tortilla in half. Add one fourth of the butter to the pan. Reduce the heat to low, cover, and cook the quesadilla on one side for a minute or two, then turn and cook on the second side until the cheese is melted. Keep warm in a low oven while cooking the remaining quesadillas.

To make a salsa, combine the remaining charred chiles with the tomato, and lime juice in a blender. Add salt and chopped cilantro to taste.

MORE PEAR SANDWICHES

Melted Brie and Comice on Sourdough Walnut Bread

Slice sourdough walnut bread into ¹/₂-inch slices. Place thin slices of fresh Comice pear on the bread and top with sliced Brie. Grill under a broiler until the Brie just begins to melt. Garnish with watercress leaves.

Pear, Pork, and Chipotle Sandwich

Between 2 slices of sourdough, layer a generous helping of thin-sliced roast pork, pieces of canned chipotle chile, and fresh ripe pear slices.

Poached Bartlett and Mascarpone on Toasted Ciabatta *(pictured below)*

Spread a generous amount of mascarpone cheese over a slice of toasted ciabatta bread. Top with a pear half that has been poached in white wine flavored with vanilla and cloves. (See page 130 for poaching instructions.)

THREE-MINUTE PEAR OATMEAL

SERVES 1

Undoubtedly, the dish I've made most in this collection has been this 3-minute microwave breakfast. Instantly, the cooked pear juices blend with the whole grain to make plain oatmeal sweet and flavorful.

$1/2$ CUP MILK

$1/2$ CUP OLD-FASHIONED OATMEAL

1 RIPE PEAR, PEELED, CORED, AND CHOPPED

$1/3$ CUP WATER

$1/8$ TEASPOON SALT

CREAM AND BROWN SUGAR OR HONEY
   FOR SERVING

Combine the milk, oatmeal, and chopped pear with the water and salt in a microwave-safe bowl, leaving plenty of head room. Microwave on high for 2 to 3 minutes, or according to your oatmeal brand directions. Stir, then add the cream and brown sugar or honey to taste.

BROILED BREAKFAST ANJOUS

SERVES 4

Preheat the broiler. Peel and halve 4 ripe Anjou pears. Scoop out the cores with a melon baller. Place the halves cut side down on a broiling pan lined with aluminum foil and baste them lightly with $1/4$ cup maple syrup. Broil for 5 minutes. Turn the pears, placing 1 tablespoon butter in each core hole, and baste again with maple syrup. Broil for another 3 to 5 minutes, or until the pears are tender. Serve on pancakes or waffles, or as a sweet side dish with eggs. Spoon on the basting syrup from the pan.

D'ANJOU-CRANBERRY CRISP

SERVES 8

This easy pecan-topped pear crisp is enlivened with tart dried cranberries, which unlike their fresh counterparts, are available year-round. Don't be afraid to use hard, just-bought pears. The texture and flavor of not-yet-ripe pears improves with cooking.

2 1/2 POUNDS ANJOU OR BOSC PEARS, CORED, PEELED, AND CHOPPED (5 CUPS)

1 CUP DRIED CRANBERRIES

PECAN TOPPING

3/4 CUP ALL-PURPOSE FLOUR

2/3 CUP PACKED LIGHT BROWN SUGAR

1 TEASPOON GROUND NUTMEG

1/2 CUP (1 STICK) COLD BUTTER, CHOPPED

1/2 CUP ROLLED OATS

1 CUP COARSELY CHOPPED PECANS OR WALNUTS

HEAVY CREAM, WHIPPED, OR VANILLA ICE CREAM

Preheat the oven to 350°. Combine the pears, cranberries, and granulated sugar in a mixing bowl. Transfer to a 9 x 13 inch baking dish and distribute evenly.

Mix the flour, brown sugar, and nutmeg in a medium bowl. Cut the butter into the flour mixture until it resembles coarse crumbs. Mix in the pecans and oatmeal. Sprinkle evenly over the fruit. Bake for 35 to 45 minutes, until the fruit is soft when pierced with the blade of a knife and the top is golden brown. Serve warm in bowls with heavy cream or ice cream.

PEAR DUTCH BABY WITH LINK SAUSAGE

SERVES 6

This hearty breakfast comes from the Northwest Pear Bureau in Medford, Oregon, a terrific source of pear recipes on the Internet. Visit them at www.usapears.com.

1 CUP UNBLEACHED ALL-PURPOSE FLOUR

1 CUP MILK

2 EGGS

1/2 TEASPOON SALT

1/4 CUP BUTTER

8 OUNCES PORK LINK SAUSAGE

2 BOSC PEARS, PEELED, CORED, AND CUT INTO 1/2-INCH SLICES

1/4 TEASPOON GROUND CINNAMON

Preheat the oven to 400°. Combine the flour, milk, eggs, and salt; blend until smooth in a blender or beat with a rotary beater.

Melt 2 tablespoons of the butter in a 10-inch ovenproof skillet. Pour in the batter. Bake for 20 minutes. Meanwhile, brown the sausages in another skillet. Drain the sausages and pour off the drippings from the pan. Add the remaining butter. Sauté the pears for 2 or 3 minutes over medium heat. Sprinkle with the cinnamon. Arrange the pear slices and sausages on top of the partially baked Dutch baby. Bake for an additional 5 to 10 minutes, or until browned. Serve immediately.

Pear Upside-Down Cake,
page 122

PEAR UPSIDE-DOWN CAKE

SERVES 8

A wonderfully rich dessert (pictured on the previous page) from Lindsey Shere, celebrated pastry chef at Chez Panisse.

5 FIRM, RIPE BOSC, WINTER NÉLIS, FRENCH BUTTER, OR BARTLETT PEARS

4 TABLESPOONS UNSALTED BUTTER

3/4 CUP PACKED BROWN SUGAR

2 TO 4 TABLESPOONS PECAN OR WALNUT HALVES

1/2 CUP SALTED BUTTER AT ROOM TEMPERATURE

1 CUP GRANULATED SUGAR

2 EGG YOLKS

1 TEASPOON VANILLA EXTRACT

1/2 CUP MILK

1 1/2 CUPS UNBLEACHED ALL-PURPOSE FLOUR

1/4 TEASPOON SALT

2 TEASPOONS BAKING POWDER

2 EGG WHITES

1/4 TEASPOON CREAM OF TARTAR

OPTIONAL TOPPING

1/2 CUP HEAVY CREAM

1 TEASPOON SUGAR

1/4 TEASPOON VANILLA EXTRACT

Preheat the oven to 350°. Core, peel, and slice the pears. Melt the unsalted butter and brown sugar in the bottom of a 9-inch square cake pan that is at least 2 inches deep. Fan the pear slices over the butter mixture in a circle (see photo, pages 120–121) and put the nuts, rounded side down, in the spaces between the pears.

Cream the salted butter with the sugar until very light and fluffy. Beat in the egg yolks well. Add the vanilla to the milk. Mix the flour, salt, and baking powder. Add the flour mixture alternately with the milk mixture, beginning and ending with the flour, until just combined. Beat the egg whites until foamy;

add the cream of tartar and beat until the whites hold softly rounded peaks.

Fold the egg whites into the batter just until combined and spread the batter over the fruit in the pan. Bake until the cake springs back in the center, 50 minutes to 1 hour. Let stand in the pan for 5 to 10 minutes, then turn out onto a cake plate. If using the topping, whip the cream, sugar, and vanilla together. Replace any fruit that sticks to the pan and serve the cake, while still warm, with the cream.

OLD WORLD STUFFED BAKED PEARS

ENGLISH PASTRY STUFFED PEARS

Cut eight $2 \frac{1}{2}$ by 10-inch strips of pie pastry (or use one 17.3-ounce package of frozen puff pastry). For each pear, lay two pastry strips perpendicular to make a cross. Moisten the pastry with a few drops of water where they intersect and gently press together to seal. Peel and core the pears, leaving the stems intact. Place 1 tablespoon of brown sugar mixed with $\frac{1}{4}$ teaspoon each of ground ginger and cinnamon into each cavity. Set one stuffed pear in the center of each pastry cross. Using a knife, taper the pastry ends to points. Moisten the ends of the pastry strips with a few drops of water. Fold the pastry strips up around the pear. Pinch the moistened edges together to seal at the top. Repeat for the remaining 3 pears. Bake for 25 minutes at 350°, or until golden brown.

The pleasure of taste is located in the tongue and palate, although often it begins not there, but in memory.

—ISABEL ALLENDE, *APHRODITE*
(NEW YORK: HARPER COLLINS, 1998)

DRIED PEAR AND ANISE OATMEAL COOKIES

MAKES 30 LARGE COOKIES

These thin golden cookies, both chewy and crisp, are an elegant variation on the old standard. Use plump golden dried pears (the sulfured variety) for this recipe. Other varieties are too tough. Samantha Beers, who created this recipe, recommends serving these cookies with vanilla or coffee ice cream.

- 1/2 CUP BUTTER
- 1 HEAPING CUP DRIED PEARS, CUT INTO 1/4 -INCH CHUNKS OR A LITTLE LARGER
- 1 TABLESPOON ANISEED
- 1 CUP SUGAR
- 1 EGG
- 2 TABLESPOONS HONEY
- 1/2 TEASPOON ALMOND EXTRACT (OPTIONAL)
- 1 CUP PLUS 2 TABLESPOONS UNBLEACHED ALL-PURPOSE FLOUR
- 1 TEASPOON BAKING SODA
- 1/2 TEASPOON SALT
- 2 CUPS BABY OATS

Preheat the oven to 350°. In a 4-quart saucepan, melt the butter. Turn off the heat. Add each of the remaining ingredients to the pan, stirring well after each addition. Spoon heaping tablespoonfuls of batter onto a nonstick or greased cookie sheet 2 inches apart. Bake for 10 to 13 minutes, or until golden brown. They are good gooey, as well as dark and crisper.

BAKED CARAMEL COMICE WITH PECANS OR ALMONDS

SERVES 6

According to Chez Panisse pastry chef Lindsey Shere, this recipe is very simple, but the flavors of the ripe Comice combine wonderfully with the smooth, rich caramel, making a superb dessert more delicious than the sum of its parts.

- **3 LARGE, VERY RIPE COMICE PEARS**
- **3 TABLESPOONS UNSALTED BUTTER**
- **3 TABLESPOONS SUGAR**
- **1/2 CUP HEAVY CREAM**
- **1 TO 2 TABLESPOONS PECANS OR ALMONDS, LIGHTLY TOASTED AND CHOPPED**

Preheat the oven to 375°. Halve, core, and peel the pears. Put the pears, rounded side down, in a flame-proof dish, such as an enameled iron gratin dish. Cut the butter into bits and distribute them over the pear halves. Sprinkle with the sugar and put the dish in the oven. Bake 20 to 30 minutes, basting occasionally with the juices. The pears are ready if tender when pierced in their thickest part with a sharp knife.

Remove the pears from the dish, allowing all the juice to drain back into it and adding any of the undissolved sugar still remaining in the pear cavities. Set the dish over high heat and cook, stirring constantly, until the mixture turns a light caramel color. It will look very thick and bubbly because of the butter and pear juice in it. Pour in the cream and bring to a boil. Cook until the sauce is smooth. It will darken and turn a rich brown when you pour in the cream.

Serve a pear half to each person with some of the sauce spooned over it. Sprinkle with the nuts.

MORAGA PEAR PIE

SERVES 6

This blue ribbon recipe comes from 82 year old Jean Podell who won Moraga, California's pear recipe contest. The town, which was built in the last hundred years on Bartlett orchards, still has many producing trees along its bike trail and open spaces. In 1999, Moraga organized a community harvest and its first annual Moraga Pear Festival to celebrate its history (for information see page 153–154).

1 UNBAKED PREPARED PIE SHELL FOR OPEN FACE PIE, OR USE **2** SHELLS FOR A TWO CRUST PIE

5-6 LARGE BARTLETT PEARS TO FILL PIE SHELL, PEELED, CORED, AND SLICED

1 CUP SUGAR

1/4 CUP BUTTER, MELTED AND COOLED

4 TABLESPOONS FLOUR

2 EGGS

1 TEASPOON VANILLA

Preheat the oven to 375°.

Fill the pie shell with the pear slices. For an open face pie, arrange the slices in circular spirals. In a small bowl, beat together the sugar, butter, flour and eggs. Pour over the pears. Place the pie on a cookie sheet and bake for 15 minutes. Reduce the oven temperature to 350 and bake 1 hour. Cover loosely with foil to prevent over browning during the last 1/2 hour of cooking time. Serve warm.

CASSIS-PEAR CLAFOUTI

SERVES 8

This warm French country pear pudding is not only elegant, but each serving has only about 100 calories. Start several hours ahead to let the rich cassis soak into the pears.

4 RIPE PEARS, PEELED, CORED WITH A MELON BALLER, AND QUARTERED

1/3 CUP CASSIS (SEE NOTE)

1 TABLESPOON FRESH LEMON JUICE

4 LARGE EGGS

1/2 CUP SUGAR

1 CUP LOW-FAT MILK

3/4 CUP UNBLEACHED ALL-PURPOSE FLOUR

2 TEASPOONS GRATED LEMON ZEST

2 TEASPOONS VANILLA EXTRACT

PINCH OF SALT

CONFECTIONERS' SUGAR FOR DUSTING

Preheat the oven to 350°. In a bowl, combine the pears, cassis, and lemon juice. Marinate at least 1 hour. Spray a 10-inch round baking pan with vegetable-oil cooking spray, sprinkle a little sugar on the bottom, and arrange the drained pears with the necks pointing towards the center. Reserve the marinade.

Combine the eggs and sugar and beat until a pale lemon color. Add the milk, flour, lemon zest, vanilla, and salt. Beat well and pour the batter over the pears. Bake 1 hour, or until the clafouti is puffed and golden brown. Sprinkle with confectioners' sugar and serve immediately, with the remaining marinade used as a sauce.

NOTE: FOR A NONALCOHOLIC SUBSTITUTE, USE THE FRESH RASPBERRY SAUCE ON PAGE 131.

ANISE RED PEAR TART

SERVES 6

Bright red poached pear slices on a golden crust make this tart especially gorgeous. To get a good rich red-wine color to the pears, let them sit in the poaching liquid overnight, or at least for 4 hours.

RED WINE POACHING LIQUID

3 CUPS DRY RED WINE

$1/2$ CUP PACKED BROWN SUGAR

1 TEASPOON ANISEED

1 VANILLA BEAN, SPLIT, OR **1** TEASPOON
    VANILLA EXTRACT

4 CLOVES

ZEST OF $1/2$ LEMON, CUT INTO $1/2$-INCH STRIPS

7 LARGE BOSC PEARS, PEELED, CORED,
    AND CUT INTO $1/2$-INCH SLICES

SHORT CRUST PASTRY

1 CUP BLEACHED ALL-PURPOSE FLOUR

$1/4$ TEASPOON GRATED LEMON ZEST

$1/2$ CUP SALTED BUTTER, CUT IN PIECES

1 TABLESPOON WATER

$1/2$ TEASPOON ALMOND EXTRACT

MINT SPRIGS FOR GARNISH (OPTIONAL)

To make the poaching liquid, combine the red wine, brown sugar, aniseed, cloves, vanilla bean or extract, and lemon zest in a large pan. Bring to a full boil. Add the pear slices and reduce heat to a simmer for 5 minutes, or until the pears are barely tender. Remove the pears from the heat. Marinate the pears for 4 hours or overnight, turning them so they color evenly.

To make the pastry, mix the flour, sugar, and lemon zest. Work the butter into the flour mixture with your fingers until crumbly. Add the water and almond extract and mix until the dough forms a ball. Cover and refrigerate for 30 minutes. Press the dough into the bottom and up the sides of a 10 $1/2$-inch tart pan.

Preheat the oven to 375°. Remove the pear slices from the liquid with a slotted spoon and place them on the shell in a spiral. Boil the poaching liquid until thick and baste the pears. Bake for 25 minutes, or until light brown. Cool for 20 minutes and serve with whipped cream and a garnish of mint.

PEAR POACHING IDEAS

POACHING LIQUIDS

PEARS IN ESPRESSO

Instead of wine, try 2 cups espresso or strong coffee, 2 tablespoons Kahlúa, and a cinnamon stick.

NONALCOHOLIC POACHED PEARS

Use white grape juice (muscat is especially good), apple cider, or cranberry juice. Balance the sweetness with some lemon or orange zest. For a nut liqueur substitute, flavor with Torani hazelnut syrup. A simple poaching method uses only water, lemon, and sugar.

POACHING HINTS

If the liquid does not cover the pears, add a little water. To keep pears submerged, cover with a clean dish towel.

POACHING SPICES

Other than the traditional cinnamon, clove, and vanilla, try spicing up your poaching liquids with some variations that appeal to you. Try a few peppercorns, a 2-inch piece of fresh ginger, or $1/4$ cup chopped candied ginger. One recipe even calls for 2 whole bulbs of garlic. Other variations include Chinese five-spice powder, cardamom seeds, or coriander seeds. Zests from lemons, oranges, or tangerines are also good.

LIQUEURS AS FLAVORING

Add 2 tablespoons of a favorite liqueur to your poaching liquid, or add it after you have boiled the liquid down into a sauce. Favorite additions are pear eau-de-vie, Grand Marnier, Fra Angelico, kirsch, or brandy.

TOPPINGS

CRÈME FRAÎCHE

Makes $1^1/_2$ cups

Crème fraîche is available at some supermarkets, but if unavailable it can be made 1 to 2 days in advance. Warm 1 cup heavy whipping cream to about 85 degrees. Remove from heat and mix in 2 tablespoons buttermilk. Cover and let stand in a warm, draft-free area for 1 to 2 full days or until slightly thickened. Sweeten with 1 to 2 tablespoons of sugar if desired. Refrigerate until ready to use.

SABAYON

(Custard sauce, also called Zabaglione)

In the top of a double boiler, add 6 extra large egg yolks, $^1/_2$ cup of poaching liquid or white wine, and 1 to 3 tablespoons of sugar to taste. Whisk until the mixture becomes thick and light yellow. Remove from heat and continue to beat until cool. Fold in $1^1/_2$ cups of heavy cream and beat until peaks form.

RASPERRY SAUCE

Combine $1^1/_2$ cups fresh rasperries, 1 tablespoon cassis or liquer, and $^1/_4$ cup confectioner's sugar in a blender. Press through a coarse sieve to remove the seeds and pulp. Serve at room temperature.

CHOCOLATE SAUCE (SEE P.136)

GARNISHES

Elegant whole poached pears deserve a pampered presentation. Try topping with lavender blossoms, a tropical hibiscus flower, a sprig of mint, slivered almonds, or thin slices of candied ginger.

CASSIS SECKEL CHARLOTTE TORTE

SERVES 12

This elegant special-occasion torte comes from Masse's Pastries in Berkeley, California. Be sure to start a day in advance or the rich blackberry color will not soak through the pears. You'll need parchment paper and a 9-inch torte ring.

POACHED PEARS

2 CINNAMON STICKS

1/2 VANILLA BEAN

1 1/2 CUPS SUGAR

3 CUPS WATER

1/2 CUP PURÉED FRESH BLACK CURRANTS

7 FIRM, RIPE SECKEL PEARS (A SMALL VARIETY)

20 LADYFINGER BISCUITS

PEAR SABAYON

1/4 CUP WATER

3 TABLESPOONS SUGAR

2 TABLESPOONS EAU-DE-VIE (PEAR LIQUEUR)

5 EGG YOLKS

1/3 CUP SUGAR

1/2 CUP PEAR NECTAR

1 VANILLA BEAN (SCRAPINGS ONLY)

3 1/2 SHEETS GELATIN, SOFTENED IN COLD WATER AND DRAINED WELL

3/4 CUP HEAVY WHIPPING CREAM, LIGHTLY WHIPPED

CASSIS MOUSSE

4 EGG WHITES

1/2 CUP SUPERFINE SUGAR

4 SHEETS GELATIN, SOFTENED IN COLD WATER AND DRAINED WELL

1/2 CUP BLACK CURRANT PURÉE, ROOM TEMPERATURE

1/2 CUP HEAVY WHIPPING CREAM, LIGHTLY WHIPPED

To make the poached pears, in a 2-quart saucepan, bring all the ingredients except the pears to a slow simmer. Peel, stem, and halve the pears, and neatly scoop out the seeds with a melon baller. Place the pears in the simmering syrup and cook until a knife goes through with ease. If your pears are ripe, check after 5 minutes. If they are unripe they may need 10 or even 15 minutes. Marinate the pears in the poaching liquid, in the refrigerator, for 24 hours, to absorb color. The liquid should cover the pears. Add a bit of water, if necessary. When the color has evenly soaked through the pears, remove them from the liquid and pat dry.

To make the sabayon, bring the water and sugar to a boil. Let cool. Add 2 tablespoons eau-de-vie. Set aside.

In a stainless steel or copper pot over a double boiler, whisk the egg yolks, sugar, pear nectar, and vanilla until lightly cooked. Remove from the heat.

(continued next page)

Add the gelatin and the eau-de-vie. Place the bowl over ice water, whisking until cool. Fold in the whipped cream.

To make the mousse, whip the eggs until they form stiff peaks. Slowly add superfine sugar and continue whipping until stiff but not dry.

In a bowl, heat the gelatin over a double boiler with $1/4$ of the purée until dissolved. Remove from the heat and add the rest of the purée. Carefully fold this mixture into the meringue. Then fold in the whipped cream gently.

To make the torte, wrap a flat sheet pan in plastic wrap. Wave the sheet pan 2 feet above stove burner to tighten the wrap. Place the 9-inch torte ring on top of the wrapped sheet pan. Place the pears, flat-side down in a pattern, leaving at least $1/4$ inch between the pears and the ring. This allows the filling to spread.

Pour the sabayon over the arranged pears, being careful not to disrupt the pears. Place I ladyfinger biscuit over the sabayon, then pour more sabayon over it. Refrigerate while preparing the cassis mousse.

Place the cassis mousse on top of the refrigerated biscuit layer of the torte. Lightly soak the second round biscuit with the sabayon, invert onto the mousse. Place the tort in the freezer for approximately $1/2$ hour.

Invert the torte onto a serving platter. While the torte is still semifrozen, glaze the top with a boiled apricot jelly or strained jam.

Remove the torte ring by heating with a kitchen towel dampened with hot water. It should slide off easily.

Place ladyfingers around the side of the cake, using I8 to 20, or less if you use the larger packaged ladyfingers. Garnish the top with a few poached pears.

RED POACHED BOSCS IN JELLED WINE

SERVES 6

Pears poached in wine have been a favorite in Europe for centuries. This recipe sets an elegant poached Bosc in its own dish of molded wine gelatin. It is surprisingly rich, and low in calories if one goes easy with the whipping cream. Use a good wine, like a fragrant Beaujolais or a fruity zinfandel that is not too sweet.

6 CUPS RED WINE POACHING LIQUID (PAGE 130; DOUBLE THE RECIPE)

6 WHOLE BOSC PEARS, CORED AND PEELED, WITH STEM INTACT

2 ENVELOPES PLAIN GELATIN

1 CUP HEAVY CREAM

^{1}/4 TEASPOON VANILLA EXTRACT

Bring the poaching liquid to a boil in a tall saucepan. Simmer for 5 minutes, stirring until the sugar in the poaching liquid is dissolved. Stand the whole pears in the liquid and simmer, covered, for about 20 minutes, or until tender. (See photo on page 88.) Allow the pears to cool in their liquid for 20 minutes, then transfer them to a plate using a slotted spoon.

Strain the poaching liquid into a medium saucepan and add enough water to make 6 cups. Sprinkle the gelatin over the liquid and let stand for 5 minutes. Heat the mixture until the gelatin is dissolved. Pour ^{1}/2-cup servings into each of 6 dessert cups. Chill the wine gelatin until it is thick but not set. Place a pear in the thickened gelatin in each cup and chill until firmly set, about 4 hours. Remove the pears from the refrigerator 15 minutes before serving. Whip together the cream and vanilla and add a dollop of the soft whipped cream to the dish with the pear.

POIRE BELLE HÉLÈNE

SERVES 6

This classic French recipe stands a poached pear in ice cream topped with chocolate sauce like a sundae. A low-fat frozen yogurt can also be used. Use a tall, elegantly shaped, and long-stemmed poaching pear like the Bosc.

POACHED PEARS

1 CUP SUGAR

3 CUPS WHITE WINE OR WHITE GRAPE JUICE

3 CUPS WATER

ZEST OF 1 ORANGE, IN 1 BY 3-INCH STRIPS

1 CINNAMON STICK

8 WHOLE CLOVES

2 TEASPOONS VANILLA EXTRACT

6 SLIGHTLY UNDERRIPE BOSC PEARS, PEELED AND CORED, WITH STEMS INTACT

CHOCOLATE SAUCE

1/3 CUP HEAVY CREAM

1/3 CUP FRA ANGELICO LIQUEUR

1/4 CUP SUGAR

PINCH OF SALT

8 OUNCES SHAVED SEMISWEET CHOCOLATE OR CHOCOLATE CHIPS

1 1/2 CUPS VANILLA ICE CREAM OR LOW-FAT FROZEN YOGURT, SOFTENED, FOR SERVING.

To make the poached pears, combine all the ingredients except the pears in a nonaluminum Dutch oven or soup pot. Bring to a boil, stirring to dissolve the sugar. Add the peeled pears, stem side up, and simmer for 20 minutes, or until the pears are just tender. (Ripe pears will cook much quicker.) Remove the pears from the poaching liquid with a slotted spoon and regfrigerate for at least 2 hours. The poaching liquid can be stored and reused.

To make the chocolate sauce, bring the cream, liqueur, sugar, and salt to a boil in a saucepan. Remove from heat, add the chocolate, and cover. After 3 minutes, blend in the chocolate until the sauce is smooth. (The sauce can be prepared several days ahead and chilled.)

To assemble, warm the chocolate sauce, if chilled, over low heat or in a double boiler. If it is too thick, add a few drops of cream. Place a large spoonful of vanilla ice cream in each dessert cup. Stand a chilled pear in the ice cream and spoon the warm chocolate sauce over the pears. Serve immediately, with your best silver spoons. *C'est merveilleux!*

OVEN-DRIED PEARS

MAKES 1 CUP

In a slow oven, pear slices will shrivel as the outside dries, and the meaty insides become soft, chewy, and caramelized. The drier the fruit, the more preserved it is, but dried pears do not have the long shelf life that canned or pickled pears have. Although fresh pears cannot be frozen, because their water content separates, dried pears will keep for weeks in the freezer.

**3 BARTLETT, BOSC, OR ANJOU PEARS,
OR 5 TO 6 SECKELS**

1 TABLESPOON SUGAR

Preheat the oven to 225°. Cut each pear lengthwise into halves. Remove the stems, seeds, and fibrous bits that run along the core. Slice the halves lengthwise, into 1/4-inch-thick (or less) pieces.

Line the pan with parchment paper to avoid sticking or purchase a special reusable baking mat with a nonstick coating. Place the slices on the pan at least 1/2 inch apart and sprinkle with the sugar.

Bake for 1 1/2 to 2 1/2 hours, or until the pears are shriveled around the edges and slightly chewy. Juices that the pears release can be basted back on to the pears while they cook. Store the pears in an airtight container in the refrigerator, or freeze in self-sealing plastic bags. Frozen pears can be warmed in a preheated 200° oven for 10 minutes, or until soft.

NOTE: DRIED PEARS CAN BE CUT INTO PIECES AND BAKED IN BREADS, MUFFINS, AND COOKIES. FOR AN EVOCATIVE AND COLORFUL GARNISH IN DESSERTS AND SALADS, USE LONG SLICES OF DRIED PEAR WITH THE STEM ATTACHED. AS A SNACK, TRY DRIED PEARS TOPPED WITH A PIECE OF CANDIED GINGER.

HOT TAMARIND AND DRIED-PEAR CHUTNEY

MAKES 2¹/₂ CUPS

For over fifteen years, I've enjoyed my neighbor's hot and spicy fruit chutney. Margaret is of Indian descent, but grew up in Fiji, where fruits are dried on rooftops. On any hot day you can dry fruits in the sun, and there's always the oven as a backup (see page 139). Serve this chutney with Indian food, eggs, bean soups, or as a spread for sandwiches.

2 CUPS (ABOUT 12 OUNCES) TAMARIND PODS, SHELLED AND PITTED

1¹/₂ CUPS WATER

1 CUP OLIVE OIL

¹/₄ CUP GRATED FRESH GINGER

1 ONION, CHOPPED

¹/₄ CUP MINCED GARLIC

1 TEASPOON MUSTARD SEED

1 TEASPOON CUMIN SEED

2 CUPS SUGAR

¹/₄ TEASPOON CAYENNE PEPPER OR MORE TO TASTE

2 TABLESPOONS CRUMBLED BAY LEAVES

1¹/₂ CUPS DRIED PEARS, CHOPPED INTO ¹/₄ -INCH PIECES

PINCH OF SALT

Soak the shelled and pitted tamarind in the water overnight. Remove any fibrous strands from the tamarind water. Set aside.

Heat the olive oil in a large saucepan over medium heat and sauté the ginger, onion, and garlic for 3 minutes. Add the mustard and cumin and continue to cook for another minute, stirring. Stir in the tamarind water. Add the sugar ¹/₂ cup at a time, stiring slowly. Add the cayenne and bay leaves. Reduce heat to low and simmer for 30 minutes. The sauce will thicken. Add the pears and salt and cook for 10 minutes. Remove from heat and cool.

BETTE'S PEAR CHUTNEY

MAKES 3 1/2 PINTS

Popular Bette's Ocean View Diner, in Berkeley, California, is famous for fabulous breakfasts and baked goods. This delicious savory fruit chutney is fat free and will warm up any fish, poultry, or steamed vegetables entrée.

- 2 1/2 POUNDS FIRM PEARS
- 2 ONIONS, DICED
- 2 CLOVES GARLIC, MINCED
- 1 1/2 CUPS PACKED BROWN SUGAR
- 2 CUPS CIDER VINEGAR
- 1 1/2 TABLESPOONS SALT
- 4 OUNCES CANDIED GINGER
- 1/2 TABLESPOON MUSTARD SEED
- 1/2 TEASPOON CAYENNE PEPPER
- 1/2 TEASPOON GROUND TURMERIC
- 3/4 CUP DRIED CURRANTS

Peel, core, and coarsely chop the pears. Combine the pears and all the remaining ingredients in an enameled or stainless steel pan. Bring the mixture to a gentle simmer and cook, uncovered, for about 1 1/2 hours, or until the pears are soft and the chutney has cooked down and thickened. Stir from time to time to prevent sticking. Ladle the chutney into clean, hot canning jars, leaving 1/4 inch head space, and seal with canning lids and rings. Place the jars in a boiling-water bath for 10 minutes or process according to the jar manufacturer's directions.

Gourmet Pear Preserves

MAKES 4 1/2 CUPS

This basic preserve recipe can be personalized with gourmet touches, dressed up with your own gift label, or just enjoyed at home during a brief moment of morning quiet.

3 POUNDS FIRM, RIPE PEARS WITH A STRONG PERFUME

1/2 CUP FRESH LEMON JUICE

JULIENNED ZEST OF 3 LEMONS

1/2 TO 1 CUP SUGAR, DEPENDING ON SWEETNESS OF PEARS

2 TABLESPOONS PEAR EAU-DE-VIE OR ORANGE LIQUEUR

Cook all the ingredients over medium heat, stirring occasionally, until the mixture is as thick as jam, about 25 minutes. Lower heat if mixture sticks. Skim off the foam, if present. A dash more liqueur can be added when mixture is thick, if a stronger flavor is desired.

Put into clean, sterilized canning jars, with 1/4 inch head space, and seal with canning lids and rings. Process the jars in a boiling-water bath for 10 minutes, or process according to the jar manufacturer's directions.

Pear-Ginger Preserves

Add 1 tablespoon grated fresh ginger.

Meyer Lemon Pear Preserves

Because the smaller Meyer lemons are sweeter, increase the lemon juice to 2/3 cup and use the zest of 4 lemons. Use pear eau-de-vie or brandy.

Pear-Anise Preserves

Add 1/2 teaspoon aniseed and 1 split vanilla bean during cooking.

Farmhouse Preserves

Substitute 1/2 cup maple syrup for the sugar, and add 1 teaspoon ground cinnamon and 1/4 teaspoon ground cloves. Use a dark rum or brandy.

MARK MILLER'S PEAR AND BLACK OLIVE SALSA

MAKES ABOUT 2 CUPS

This spicy, sweet salsa (pictured on page 98) is a colorful accompaniment to thin slices of grilled or roasted turkey, chicken, or quail.

- **1 TABLESPOON CANOLA OIL**
- **3 PEARS, PEELED, CORED, AND DICED**
- **1 TEASPOON SUGAR**
- **8 NIÇOISE OR KALAMATA OLIVES, PITTED AND SLICED**
- **3 PLUM TOMATOES, ROASTED AND DICED**
- **1 SMALL POBLANO CHILE, ROASTED, PEELED, SEEDED, AND DICED**
- **1 SMALL RED BELL PEPPER OR FRESH NEW MEXICO RED CHILE, ROASTED, PEELED, SEEDED, AND DICED**
- **1 TABLESPOON APPLE CIDER VINEGAR**

Heat the oil in a pan and sauté the pears with the sugar over medium-low heat for 2 minutes. Transfer to a mixing bowl. Thoroughly combine with all the remaining ingredients.

From The Great Salsa Book *by Mark Miller (Berkeley, CA: Ten Speed Press, 1994)*

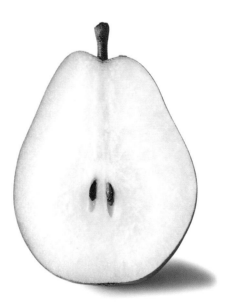

BUTTER-PEAR BUTTER

MAKES 2^1/$_2$ TO 3 CUPS

Pear butter is a smooth, flavorful spread that can be used as a sweet low-calorie alternative to butter.

- 2 POUNDS UNRIPE TO FIRM, RIPE BUTTER PEARS, CORED AND QUARTERED
- ^{1}/$_2$ CUP WHITE GRAPE JUICE OR ORANGE JUICE
- ^{1}/$_2$ CUP APPLE CIDER
- ^{1}/$_2$ CUP HONEY
- 1 VANILLA BEAN, SPLIT, OR 1 TEASPOON VANILLA EXTRACT
- 2 WHOLE CLOVES
- 1 TEASPOON GROUND CINNAMON
- ^{1}/$_2$ TEASPOON GROUND NUTMEG
- ^{1}/$_2$ TEASPOON GRATED LEMON ZEST

Bring all the ingredients to a boil. Reduce heat to low, cover, and simmer for about 30 minutes, or until the pears are soft and translucent. Stir frequently and add as little water as possible to avoid sticking. Put the mixture through a food mill or a strainer and cool.

Ginger-Pear Butter

Add 2 ^{1}/$_8$-inch slices of fresh ginger, or 4 to 5 pieces of candied ginger.

BALSAMIC PEAR VINEGAR

MAKES 3 CUPS

Add 1 pear, cored and chopped, or 1 whole fork-pierced pear, to 2 cups wine vinegar and 1 cup balsamic vinegar in a glass jar with a tight lid. Seal and store at room temperature for 2 to 4 weeks. Strain several times through cheesecloth until the vinegar is clear.

PEAR FRUIT COMPOTE

MAKES 2 1/2 CUPS

This fruit compote is rich, soft, syrupy, and colorful.

- **8 OUNCES DRIED PEARS**
- **8 OUNCES MIXED DRIED CRANBERRIES, APRICOTS, PEACHES, PRUNES, RAISINS**
- **1 1/2 CUPS WATER OR TO COVER**
- **ZEST OF 1/2 LEMON**
- **2 TABLESPOONS PEAR EAU-DE-VIE OR BRANDY (OPTIONAL)**

Place the fruits in a pan and add the water, lemon zest, and eau-de-vie, if using. Simmer for 1 1/2 hours over very low heat, or until the fruit is soft and the liquid rich and syrupy. Store in the refrigerator. Use the compote for a meat accompaniment, as a natural sugar substitute, over ice cream, or blended for a quick jam.

PEAR LEMONADE

SERVES 4

Fresh pear juice is one of the most delicious ways to enjoy pears. Most of the mixed-fruit juices marketed begin with a pear base, which is usually disguised with other flavors. If you don't have a big supply of pears or a juicer on hand, you can still enjoy a fresh pear drink with this blender lemonade. Drink immediately or the pulp will separate.

- 3/4 CUP FRESH LEMON JUICE
- 3 RIPE BUT NOT MUSHY LARGE COMICE OR BARTLETT PEARS, PEELED, CORED, AND CHOPPED
- 1 1/4 CUPS WATER
- 1/3 CUP SUGAR
- 10 ICE CUBES, CRUSHED
- 3 MINT LEAVES, CRUSHED, PLUS MINT SPRIGS FOR GARNISH

Add all the ingredients except the mint to a blender. After blending to a smooth consistency, taste for more sugar or thin with more water, if desired. Blend again. Add the crushed mint leaves. Stir and remove the leaves. Pour into stemmed glasses and garnish with a sprig of mint.

NOTE: TRY PEAR JUICE STRAIGHT UP OR MIXED WITH ANOTHER FRUIT. FAVORITE COMBINATIONS ARE TWO-THIRDS PEAR AND ONE-THIRD CANTALOUPE, AND ONE-HALF CARROT AND PEAR.

COCONUT COMICE SORBET

SERVES 6

Sasha Weiss, the pastry chef at the Millennium restaurant in San Francisco, invents elegant, delectable desserts without using any animal products (butter, milk, or honey) or refined sugars. This recipe calls for fructose, a white crystalline sweetener derived from fruit that can be obtained at natural food stores. Pear cider can be found in gourmet markets. You can substitute hard apple cider. Serve this with biscotti for a simple ending to a meal.

1 1/2 CUPS HARD PEAR CIDER

1/2 CUP LIGHT COCONUT MILK

2 TABLESPOONS PLUS 1 TEASPOON BRANDY

3/4 CUP FRUCTOSE, OR 1/2 CUP SUGAR

3 LARGE PEARS

PINCH OF SALT

Combine the cider, coconut milk, brandy, and fructose in a saucepan. Core and peel the pears, putting each pear into the liquid as soon as it is peeled, so that it will not brown. When all the pears are in the pot, cover it and place it over medium heat. Simmer for about 20 minutes, or until the pears are soft. Remove from the stove and carefully purée in a blender or food processor until smooth. Put the purée in a container and refrigerate until chilled before freezing it in an ice cream maker. You can also make this sorbet in the freezer. Put the chilled mixture in the freezer and stir it once every 20 minutes for 2 or 3 hours to achieve a soft, frozen consistency.

FOR PEAR-BERRY SORBET

Combine 1/4 cup lime juice, 1/4 cup sugar (or more, to taste), and I cup of water in a saucepan. Add 3 cored and peeled smooth-textured pears (Bartlett, Seckel, or Comice). Follow cooking, blending, and freezing directions as in previous recipe but add I pack cup fresh berries when blending.

SMOOTH MORNING SMOOTHIE

SERVES 2

These glorious, pale orange smoothies from Samantha Beers have a flowery, heady flavor perfect for brightening up a gray day. Yum!

- **1** SWEET RIPE **BARTLETT** PEAR, PEELED, CORED, AND CHOPPED
- **2** CUPS CARROT JUICE
- **2** RIPE BANANAS, PEELED AND CHOPPED
- **3** TABLESPOONS PROTEIN POWDER (SOLD IN NATURAL FOOD STORES)
- **1**-INCH-THICK PIECE FRESH GINGER, PEELED

Combine all the ingredients in a blender and blend until smooth. If you want a cold and frosty drink, add 1 cup ice to the mix. Blend then drink immediately.

HEIRLOOM TREASURES

*P*ears own a glorious, aristocratic past. With beautiful French names like Louise Bonne d'Avranches and Duchesse d'Angoulême, pears were once the dessert of kings and the pride of a gentleman's garden. But the exquisite heirlooms that were developed in cloistered European monasteries have been dismissed by twentieth-century growers because they lack the basketball-like qualities necessary for packing and shipping.

Due to disinterest and neglect, the old American orchards have been gradually erased from the landscape. California's Santa Clara Valley, one of the world's richest fruit-growing regions, is now called Silicon Valley. Its last Comice orchard has become an outlet mall. At one time hundreds of pear varieties were grown in the United States, but today a gardener will find fewer than fifty through mail order. The little White Doyenné and the other delicious heirloom pears that were once the toast of Europe have acquired a sad museumlike status: to be photographed, talked about, germ plasm tagged, and even pictured on the Internet, but never tasted. Only a handful of fruit preservationists, specialty farmerrs, and gourmet chefs know that the diverse old orchards are a disappearing national treasure. The future of these orchards lies with those able to care for them and consumers who seek out special produce.

Walking in an orchard recently, I watched my two-year-old granddaughter reach up for a fruit on the

Plant apples for your children, and pears for your grandchildren.

—FOLK SAYING

tree and saw her delight when it fell into her hands. She knew exactly what to do with it. An old orchard has a magic about it, a sort of unspoken wisdom. I like the feel of stepping on the warm, soft turned

The author's granddaughter, Deanna

earth that leaves little dirt clumps in my shoes. Perhaps the old trees hold secrets in their plasm germ, not only about their place in history, but about what makes life worth living.

Barbara Flores, a well-respected graphic designer, has created over 30 food posters for Celestial Arts which are displayed worldwide in homes, offices and restaurants, and as set pieces in films and commercials. Also an accomplished writer, Barbara is the author of **Confusion is a State of Grace** *(Hazelden Press, 1995) and* **The Great Sunflower Book** *(Ten Speed Press, 1998).*

PEAR FESTIVALS AND FRUIT SHOWS

All About Fruit Show
PORTLAND, OREGON
SECOND WEEKEND IN OCTOBER

The All About Fruit Show is sponsored by the Home Orchard Society, a nonprofit organization dedicated to preserving fruit varieties that are no longer marketed. The fruit show displays over 100 varieties of fruit and includes a fruit tasting, competitions, educational exhibits, raffles, and classes on topics such as fruit preservation, fertilizers, and soil. In addition, the Home Orchard Society's experts will identify any unknown fruit specimens that may be growing in your backyard. Contact Jerry Shroyer of the Home and Orchard Society at (503) 266-6745.

Fall Harvest Festival
SANTA CRUZ, CALIFORNIA
SECOND SATURDAY IN OCTOBER

Many varieties of organic pears and apples, grown on the University of California farm in Santa Cruz, are featured for tasting as well as samples donated by private growers in the Monterey area. Also offered are tours of the farm and orchard and advice from knowledgeable growers on fine fruit varieties.

UCSC's farm is located on campus. For information and directions, contact University of California, Center for Agroecology and Sustainable Food Systems (SASFS), 1156 High Street, Santa Cruz, CA 95064, (831) 459-4140.

Filoli Fall Festival
WOODSIDE, CALIFORNIA
SATURDAY IN LATE SEPTEMBER OR OCTOBER

Each year, approximately 1,500 members of the Friends of Filoli organization, their guests, and the general public attend the Filoli Fall Festival, featuring apple and pear tastings from the Filoli fruit collection.

Many different varieties of Filoli pears, with different harvest times, are picked, stored in the underground fruit cellar, and ripened to perfection to be ready for the Filoli guests.

Other activities include pie-baking contests, cider making, and horticultural tours of the orchard, fruit cellar, and formal gardens. Fruit questions from home gardeners are answered by University of California farm advisors. Members of the California Rare Fruit Growers demonstrate budding and grafting techniques and bring in exotic private collection fruits to taste.

Filoli Historical House and Gardens is located off Highway 280, at 86 Cañada Road, Woodside, CA 94062. For information, call (650) 364-8300. See www.filoli.org for the event schedule.

Kelseyville Pear Festival
KELSEYVILLE, CALIFORNIA
LAST SATURDAY IN SEPTEMBER

California is the leading producer of Barletts, producing over 300 thousand tons a year. To celebrate, the Kelseyville goes all out in honor of the bright yellow summer Bartlett. There's a Bartlett pie contest; Bartletts in tarts, shakes, and shish kabobs; even a Bartlett pear packing contest, which pits strong-armed packers from different packing houses in a speed race to pack two boxes of (bruiseless) pears. A parade with the reigning Pear Prince and Pear Princess (chosen on the basis of their fifth-grade essay on the importance of pears) and an entourage of bands, antique buggies, and tractors add to the fun.

Kelseyville is twenty miles east of U.S. 101, about seventy-five miles north of San Francisco, at Clear Lake. Contact Holdenried Farms at (707) 279-9022.

Moraga Pear Festival
MORAGA, CALIFORNIA
LAST SATURDAY IN SEPTEMBER (SUBJECT TO CHANGE)

Moraga sponsors a one-day event in honor of its pear orchard history. Pear pies are made from the community Bartlett harvest and locals celebrate with crafts, food booths, and a pear bake-off contest.

The festival is held at the Moraga Commons on Moraga Road, south of Highway 24. For more information, call the Moraga Park and Recreation Department (925) 631-6842.

Monticello
CHARLOTTESVILLE, VIRGINIA
AUGUST

Monticello, the colonial home of Thomas Jefferson, has a restored historical orchard that preserves some of Jefferson's favorite pear varieties, including Seckel, Crassanne, and Butter pears. The orchard, plant shop, and guided tours are available to the public from mid-April through October. Fruit tastings are scheduled in August.

Monticello is located at Virginia Road, Route 53, 2 miles southeast of Charlottesville. Dates for fruit tastings vary, and you must register and pay ahead of time. Call (804) 984-9822 or (804) 984-9844.

Pear Blossom Festival
MEDFORD, OREGON
SECOND WEEKEND IN APRIL

In April, the Rogue River Valley surrounding Medford turns white with blossoming pear trees, including the trees of Harry and David, the mail-order fruit company. Though the festival is more about community fun than about pears (with a ten-mile run, mayor's walk, food booths, parade, and pageant), scenic Medford is a good place to relax or take in the nearby first-class Ashland Shakespeare festival.

Medford is on Interstate 5, about thirty miles north of the California state line. Contact Pear Blossom Festival Office, P.O. Box 335, Medford, OR 97501, (541) 734-PEAR, or check out www.so-oregon.com/color/blossom.html.

SPECIALTY NURSERIES

Henry Leuthardt Nurseries, Inc.
Montauk Highway
Box 666-HB
East Moriches, Long Island NY
11940
(516) 878-1387
Rare rootstock varieties, Espalier techniques, and classes.

One Green World
28696 South Crammer Road
Molalla, OR 97038
(503) 651–3005
oga@cybcon.com
www.onegreenworld.com
Bareroot hierloom pears and rootstock

Raintree Nursery
391 Butts Road
Morton, WA 983566400
raintreenursery.com
Bareroot hierloom pears and rootstock

Sonoma Antique Apple Nursery
4395 Westside Road
Healdsburg, CA 95448
(707) 433–6420
(707) 433–6479 (fax)
tuyt20b@prodigy.com
Sells hierloom pear variety rootstock, custom propagation, and espaliered fruit trees.

Southmeadow Fruit Gardens
10603 Cleveland Avenue
Baroda, MI 49101
(616) 469-2865

Seed Saver's Exchange
3076 North Winn Road
Decorah, IA 52101
(319) 382–5990
(319) 382–5872 (fax)
Publishes a Fruit, Berry and Nut Inventory of fruits and nurseries.

Vintage Gardens
2833 Old Gravenstein Hwy South
Sebastopol, CA 95472
(707) 829–2035
(707) 829–9516 (fax)
www.vintagegardens.com
Espaliered hierloom pears yearround and bareroot varieties and rootstock

RESOURCES

California Rare Fruit Growers
5081 Dartmouth Avenue
Westminster, CA 92683
(714) 890-1939
www.CRFG.org
Publishes The Fruit Gardener, a bimonthly magazine

Harry and David
P.O. Box 712
Medford, OR 97501
(800) 345–5655
www.harryanddavid.com
Gift baskets, including cakes and chocolates using Royal Riviera pears.

Home Orchard Society
c/o Ted Swensen
Portland, OR
(503) 293-1468
fax (503) 977-9330
tswensen@jps.net

Nafex, North American Fruit Explorers, Inc.
PO Box 29
Lucernemines, PA 15754
Publishes Pomona, a quarterly journal devoted to superior fruit varieties.
www.nafex.org

Northwest Pear Bureau
4282 Southeast International Way
Milwalkie, OR 97222-4635
(503) 652–9720
(503) 652–9721 (fax)
www.z.usapears.com/pears

USDA National Clonal Germplasm Repository
33447 Peoria Road
Corvallis, OR 97333-2521

ACKNOWLEDGMENTS

hank you to the other two writers of this book, namely Lucy Tolmach, for contributing "Pears in the Garden," and C. Todd Kennedy, for his varietal descriptions and proofing. Their lifelong dedication to saving our fruit orchards was the true inspiration for this book. Much gratitude also to pear lovers Lindsey Shere of Chez Panisse for the foreword and to CEO/farmer Sue Naumes for her comments on the pear industry.

This unique photographic pear collection, for which the "subjects" were photographed over two growing seasons, was made possible through the generous donations of rare varieties from the Filoli Estate; Jonathan Tolmach, who harvest and ripens the Filoli pears; Sonoma Antique Apple Nursery; Goldbud Farms; Gabriel Farm; and the National Clonal Germplasm Repository in Corvallis, Oregon.

This book also belongs to photographer Susanne Kaspar for her exquisite botanical pear portraits and the beyond-the-call-of-duty pear shoots she did from markets in New York to orchards in Healdsburg, California. A thank you also to photographer Ed Gowans for capturing the scenic beauty of Oregon's orchards.

On the culinary side, the recipes of noted chefs Mark Miller, Lindsey Shere, Linda West Eckhardt, Gordon Heiss, Suzanne Adams, Caprial Pence, Bette Kroening, Sasha Weiss, and Samantha Beers put the common pear back on its gourmet pedestal.

Other contributors to thank: Dr. David Sugar of Oregon State University, Maggie Andrè of the Northwest Pear Bureau in Medford, Oregon; Doug Gosling, the Monticello Estate; Wayne David Hand, calligrapher/artist/historian; Joseph Postman of the USDA Germplasm Repository in Corvallis, Oregon; and the late Fr. Harry B. Morrison, who researched the history of the missions.

On the publishing side, I wish to thank my Ten

Speed family. I'm indebted to Phil Wood, Kirsty Melville, David Hinds, Lisa Patrizio, and my editor, Lorena Jones, who encouraged, enlightened, and gave the go-ahead. To all of you, I wish continued prosperity and an abundant harvest.

PHOTOGRAPHY & ARTWORK CREDITS

INDEX